THE PERFECT PRAYER

for the

Perfect Storm

For further information:

The Agreement Center
P.O.Box 200367 Arlington, TX 76006

www.theagreementcenter.com

First Edition
July 2016
Printed in the USA
Book Production by
Createspace

The Perfect Prayer for the Perfect Storm
ISBN 0-9703932-4-5
Published by:
Falcon Publishing

Cover concept & design by Dr. Thomas Michael

THE PERFECT PRAYER

for the

Perfect Storm

www.theagreementcenter.com
By the Author of The Agreement, The Secret and The Law of Order

DR. THOMAS MICHAEL

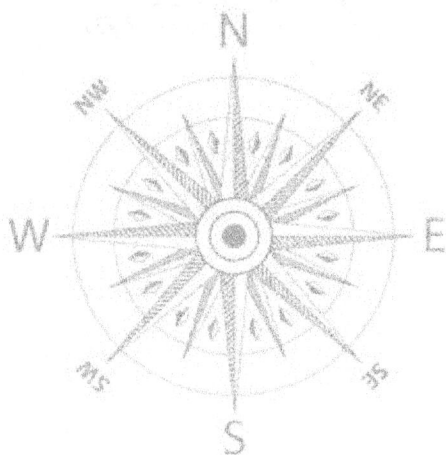

This book is dedicated to all the pastors/shepherds who pray for and watch over their sheep and fight the good fight of faith every day. To all the men and women of God who have stayed the course and still find a way to shine brightly even after all the storms they have endured.

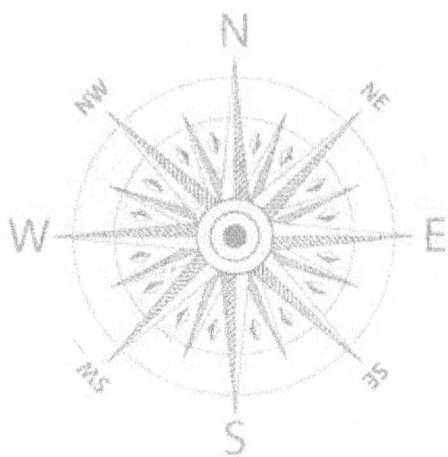

ACKNOWLEDGMENTS

I would like to thank Holy Spirit, the Shekinah glory of God, for the inspiration and revelation in this book.

To my wife, thank you for standing with me in the good times and the bad. Together, we have weathered the tempestuous grind of ministry life and grown through it all, and discovered we are strongest as a team.

To my beautiful daughter, Katherine: my angel girl, you will always be *daddy's little girl.* You're my sunshine when clouds weigh heavy overhead. *"You bring joy to my world like no other girl..."*

To my beloved son, Carrington, you are my delight! Because of you, I am able to understand a little better what the Father meant when He said, *"This is my beloved son, in whom I am well-pleased."* I am always so proud of the man you have become; even still, you will always be *"daddy's little lamb."*

To Trina, my faithful assistant, "You're my favorite grammarian." Thank you for staying in agreement and putting His will before yours. Your reward is great!

To Raymond and Soledad Edwards for your love, financial support and the special seeds you sowed to help make this book a reality and to Birdie for believing in this message even when it was just a tiny seed.

To The Agreement Center: my church, my family, my friends, my sheep. You have stood by me and with me through the many storms in the life of a pastor in passionate pursuit of the glory. You patiently waited these past five years for this book to be birthed and you never gave up on me.

To all my faithful partners and loyal readers who have stayed in the agreement and anticipated the release of this book. *Whither thou goest, I will go, whither thou lodgest, I will lodge, thy people shall be my people and thy God my God...*

"Give me a lantern, a compass and a map,
I've got to find my way to the sacred mountain.
I want to go to the place of your presence." Dr. Thomas Michael

PREFACE

There's a perfect storm brewing; the waves are crashing; the lightning strikes and searches out every peak and point on which to unleash the majesty of its power. The ship is stressed from stem to stern. The bow creaks, and the floors buckle as boards snap and fly out into the abyss of the ocean's unforgiving, cavernous depths. The captain's cries are scarcely heard above the sheets of rain pounding down on every inch of everything. "Batten down the hatches!" he cries. Suddenly, there's a small lull in the storm. The waves seem to be subsiding, and a slight calm comes over the raging sea. Then as quickly as the reprieve comes, the perfect storm hits with a mighty vengeance. The struggle is now a life and death matter. The shipmen are ready to give up and abandon ship; when out of nowhere, a break in the menacing clouds gives way to a ray of hope.

There are storms brewing all over the world. There have been 136 mass shootings in the first 164 days of 2016 in the US. There is turmoil from the land of the free to the far side of the world. Today, in Dallas, Texas, 11 policemen were wounded and 5 killed. The storm is moving closer to home.

Millions are being displaced all over the world, and refugees crowd into anything resembling a boat and risk life and limb in the hopes of escaping the storms of hatred and genocide in their war-torn countries. Their desperation calls for something more than just a simple prayer from a group of people sitting in air-conditioned churches with padded pews, and steeple crowned buildings. And still, out of this gathering of misfits comes the true cry from those who have not been swayed or moved by the wooing and pandering of the status quo. ...those who have forfeited the pleasure of self-indulgence and truly prayed the effectual fervent prayer that avails much. Those who pound the gates of heaven, for the violent take it by force. There is a remnant that is willing to push past the religious rhetoric and demand justice that can only come from the justice giver. From the one who calms the storm... From the one who walks on water... From the one who made a way from darkness to light... The one who saved us and taught us to "Pray in this manner..."

Endorsements and Testimonies

"Thus saith the LORD, 'Don't worry about hooking up with big name people, God is going to use you to lead millions into worship. People will fill stadiums to hear the message of worship."
Dr. Juanita Bynum, Evangelist/Prophetess

"People are never the same after the experience of worship with Dr. Thomas."
Dr. Zonnya, "God's Woman of Encouragement."

"The glory of God fills the house when my pastor, Dr. Thomas Michael begins to minister. He's a golden link into a glorious place with God. I have seen angels fill the sanctuary as he ministers in worship and song. Dr. Thomas is imparting to the Body of Christ what may become his greatest legacy – The Agreement. I read his manuscript in the Secret Place, my private place for meeting with the Holy Spirit daily. Truly, the Spirit has burned this divine and life changing revelation into the heart of this uncommon man of God."
Dr. Mike Murdock, Evangelist/Author

"I sat at my desk thumbing back through the manuscript sent to me by my dear friend, Dr. Thomas Michael. It looks like a swirling rainbow. Why? Bold yellow highlights, green underlines of memorable quotes, vibrant red question marks around unfamiliar words like "Phi", thick black sharpie exclamations of "Wow!" and "Ugh" framing certain revelatory truths."
Reba Rambo~McGuire, Singer/songwriter/evangelist

"The Law of Order will touch the heart of anyone who wants to understand the secrets of life and take them on a journey to God's will for all mankind."
The late, Dr. Myles E. Munroe, Bahamas Faith Ministries Nassau, Bahamas

"His musical talents and abilities far exceed anything I have ever seen on Broadway or Hollywood."
The late, Rev. Tammy Faye, "First Lady of Christian TV"

The perfect prayer for the perfect storm is something we all need. My friend, Dr. Thomas Michael was inspired to write about it. Let him encourage you and inspire you to dive into the deep places of God's presence where prayer takes us. In my experience, the highest level of

prayer is worship. As a child, growing up in a Pentecostal pastor's home, we didn't have the term worship service; we had song service and prayer service. Worship was woven into the tapestry of our prayer life. It's very much the same for me today. You may call it worship; but, it's truly a deep, beautiful secret place of prayer.
Jeff Ferguson; Singer, Songwriter, Evangelist, Pastor
Dallas, TX

"I wanted to send you a note of gratitude for your fervent prayers. They helped both Mother and me so very much. I've made HUGE strides in getting better. I simply cannot express the shear magnitude of grace and mercy ABBA Father has shown me these last few weeks. He put you, a dedicated and unstoppable servant to intercede on my behalf and to bring comfort and wisdom to my mother in her weakest moments, watching her only child suffer with cancer. Only God can give that sense of strength and peace that passes all understanding. ~ I love you."
Kim Cornelius
Houston, TX

"I realized more than ever, I needed a formula for effective prayer that could help me deal with the, sometimes, crazy and chaotic world I live in. The Perfect Prayer has helped me understand that when I pray it is simply gibberish, but when I pray according to God's will – that's where the power is! My words mean nothing unless they are in agreement with God's word."
Trina Gamez
Arlington, TX

"This teaching on the Lord's Prayer has removed the scales from my eyes, and Truth has been revealed. It's like an awakening in my soul. I was facing a situation that almost cost me my life, and I lost everything. Now, almost everything has been restored."
Ray Edwards
Haslet, TX

"The Perfect Prayer has brought such miraculous manifestations into my life. Not only has it taught me I create as I speak, but also the importance of praying and doing the will of YAHVEH. It has unlocked many possibilities for me!"
Nadia Gamez
Los Angeles, CA

"As with all your teachings this one on the perfect prayer changed my life! Your teaching and book "The Agreement" changed my marriage! Now, I know the power of agreement through prayer, especially with you, my man of God. Our agreement with YAHVEH'S word has brought my daughter through two cancers and will bring her through this third one. I shared the perfect prayer with my daughter, and I believe everything I taught her in that time has changed her; therefore, you have changed her. While in the hospital, being treated for severe complications to chemotherapy, she even prayed for a nurse with the same cancer! Without what you have taught me over the years I don't know how I would have made it through the challenges that I have gone through with my only child. I know you are always there to love, intercede, and come into agreement, and you will always be loved more than you can know for guiding me and my family through life. I truly can't imagine life without you."

Pammie Pereira
Bedford, TX

Special Thanks to my Partners

Diana Holzhey
Jessica Hudson
Jesse and Liza Reed
Anita-Louise
Andrew Flores
Jeremiah and Raquel Hare
Judy McCullough De La Garza
Erin Gomez
Racquel Rocha
Victoria Gonzalez
Raymond and Soledad Edwards
Odi Aguinaga
Stephanie Aguinaga
Pammie Pereira
Andrea Carrion

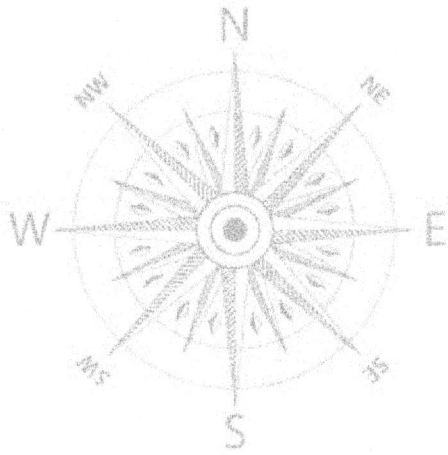

TABLE OF CONTENTS

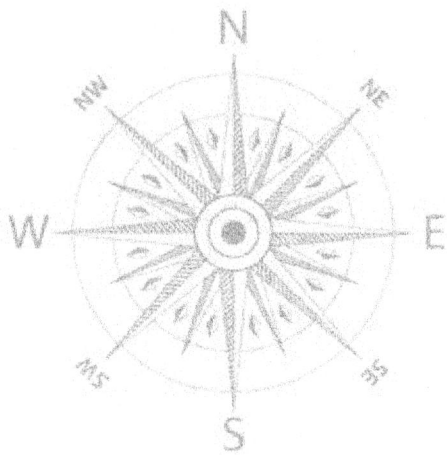

FOREWORD

Dr. Thomas has been a personal friend of mine for over 30 years. He is one of the many young men from my tenure as a youth pastor who entered into fulltime ministry. I knew him when he was Tommy, and I have watched him grow into the powerful man of God he is today.

He is faithful...
He is loyal...
He is a trusted confidant...
His character is unblemished...
His integrity is untarnished...

He has successfully pastored The Agreement Center for 28 years, which speaks volumes of his commitment and faith. His endurance is proof of his love for God and his congregation.

He is a pastor, a psalmist, an orator, an author, a musician, a songwriter, but most importantly he is a worshiper. It is out of this anointing that this revelatory masterpiece has been birthed. He has unlocked a vault of ancient mysteries that have been sealed and now revealed for such a time. The Perfect Prayer for the Perfect Storm is an expository on a topic, obviously, dear to my heart. My 30 year classic, *COULD YOU NOT TARRY ONE HOUR?* has been translated into 20 languages, and now Dr. Thomas has birthed the next great revelation! This book will change your life. This book will revolutionize how you pray and why you pray. Dr. Thomas vocalizes what many are afraid to speak. It is a pastor's handbook. Fearlessly, he weaves together wisdom, revelation and practical lessons for a more powerful prayer life. This book will reveal the Father's heart and ultimately His will.

Dr. Larry Lea
Apostle of Prayer

"Stand at the crossroads and look; ask for the ancient paths, ask where the good way is, and walk in it, and you will find rest for your souls..." Jeremiah 6:16

Chapter One
The Introduction

We can all use a little help and direction when we get lost and confused by the chaos of life. Remember when as children, we would dance around *indoors* singing, "Rain, rain, go away; come again some other day?" All the while hoping the rain would stop so we could take the fun outdoors? Sometimes, rainy days can bring us down. As a child, it represented the epitome of the worst day, but as an adult, I learned to recognize and appreciate its profound value. Now, I love rainy days; they invoke something inside of my spirit. I feel more creative when it's overcast and love when the raindrops hit my body on a scorching hot day.

Rain is what keeps everything green and causes trees to grow and provides nutrients to the plant that gives birth to a beautiful flower. Water is the essence of life! Water is God's formula He created for His creation. Most of us spent nine months inside our mother's womb floating around in water. Water increases the blood supply in our bodies; it improves brain function and is essential to maintaining good health. One of the first things that humans stranded at sea experience is dementia because the brain becomes dehydrated. You get the picture: water, rain, dew. Moisture in whatever form is essential to life! We cannot survive without water; and yet, a rainy day for many is cause for sadness, gloom and even depression. I have to admit there is something melancholic about a rainy day. One of the songs I heard as a child and am quite familiar with says, "Rainy days and Mondays always get me down..." I see and hear the pitter-patter of the rain on the windows of my study, and somehow I know something great is about to happen!

It seems as though it has rained for forty days and forty nights because we have endured a deluge of rain for the past month and a half. Flooding has occurred in many areas around the great state of Texas. Reports show that the random floods are not only confined to Texas, but all over the United States, and these floods and hurricanes have left a path of devastation and destruction in their wake. I can only wonder what kind of prayers a person enduring such loss could utter at this very moment. What could I or anybody else say to these people to bring about healing over the loss of their loved ones, their homes and their serenity?

The countless families devastated by water, the very source of life, have become victims of these beautiful, fluffy, snow-white clouds turned into dark, ominous thunderhead-like monsters pounding down their wrath with no warning to anyone below. It is at these moments we recognize the fragility of life and realize how quickly life's problems can thrust us into the perfect storm. And the only way through a perfect storm is by knowing how to navigate through it. Storms will come, but some storms can and will be averted by simply knowing the One who can calm the storm.

As you read through the pages of this book, you will soon learn that prayer is not as vague as one may think. The ambiguity will become the basis for an "aha" moment that will lead you into a clear understanding of how to pray and how to properly approach God. Praying the right prayer at the right time can produce the blessed life everyone longs for.

We have all endured or will endure a perfect storm in our lives. Jesus had many dealings with perfect storms. The most famous or most well known of the storms Jesus dealt with is found in the fourth chapter of Mark. The disciples were taking Jesus to a place where he could rest after watching him perform many miracles. Tired and exhausted from ministry, Jesus retires to the sleeping

2

quarters of the boat while the disciples man the ship. Perhaps, this is a signpost letting us know what can happen when we, and not the Savior, are at the helm.

Doesn't it always seem that when you need peace and quiet the most, the perfect storm is brewing not far behind a cloud or two? Soon after they set sail, Jesus falls asleep with the disciples at the helm, and a perfect storm appears out of nowhere and swallows up the tiny vessel crashing it here and there. Surely, these men traveling with the Savior had some experience with storms – many of them were fishermen. Certainly, this short trek across a small body of water was not their first squall, and now it seemed that it would be their last. And yet, by the sheer fact the Son of God was in the boat with them, somehow they knew this was not just any storm; it was the perfect storm!

Mark 4:37-40 (ESV) And a great windstorm arose, and the waves were breaking into the boat, so that the boat was already filling… And they woke him and said to him, "Teacher, do you not care that we are perishing?"

The waves churned and tossed the small boat to the point that Jesus finally decides to come out of his peaceful sleep. How could anyone sleep quietly through a raging storm? Nevertheless, Jesus comes up from the stern, and confronts the raging storm, heavy winds blowing, sheets of rain slapping down upon him, and he shouts over the loud noise to his disciples, "Have you still no faith?" Perceiving they were about to perish, with full trust and confidence in His Father, he says, "Shhhhhh, peace be still!" With one quick word, one sharp gesture, the great storms subside, and the sea becomes calm once again. Jesus rebuked the storm. The words *"be still"* actually mean to shush or to shame, to stop the mouth, make speechless, reduce to silence. Imagine the disciples, who walked side by side with Jesus: the Messiah, the chosen one, the anointed one, the one who could perceive their thoughts, and still, their faith was lackluster and in need of some correction, direction and focus.

I have stood on the shoreline of the Sea of Galilee and led worship for those who traveled with us. It is a peaceful body of water that caused me to be somewhat incredulous that a storm with 150-foot waves could come out of this sea. Our tour guide explained how waves of this magnitude can form out of nowhere because the sea sits at the base of two hills. When under perfect circumstances,

3

the wind can channel between these two hills and create gusts of winds that result in the perfect storm.

There are a couple of things we must take note of, even if we are people of faith, who believe in prosperity and divine health. Even Jesus was subject to life's limitations and certainly had his fair share of perfect storms. A couple years later, he would face his greatest storm, one that would rear its ugly head at the top of a mount called Calvary. This perfect storm would cost him his very life.

Even as I write this, there are many perfect storms brewing all over the world. There is an economic storm brewing that will make what we've been through in the past economic depressions feel like a stroll in the park. There are more and more diseases cropping up every day presenting us with perfect storms that could lead to a compromise in our health systems giving way to epidemic catastrophes. You may be facing a perfect storm in your own health.

The perfect storm comes in the form of an incendiary divorce or separation. It can appear in your finances and wipe you clean of your life's savings. There are perfect storms brewing at every turn, but we have not been left to deal with them alone. Jesus is in our boat, and as long as he is with us, the boat will not go down! The Perfect Prayer for the Perfect Storm is just a page turn away, so I speak to the perfect storm in your life and say, "Shhh, peace be still!"

God looks at the intent of each cry, each request, each prayer we utter. Prayer is more than words in the form of requests with the hopes of hitting the jackpot. Motive, faith, trust, trust, trust, and more trust are key ingredients to the Perfect Prayer. Can one ever be truly certain that the motive of prayer is absolutely in right standing with God and His perfect will? You're going to read a lot about God's perfect will, perfect storms, perfect prayers, perfect timing because everything God does is perfect! There is no accident in the life of a person of destiny; it is part of God's perfect design. We are people of destiny, not opportunists. An opportunist waits for a breach or fault in someone else's misfortune to get his foot in the door. A person of destiny has the faith and trust that God is going to bring about what He has promised by simply staying on the path of purpose.

Chapter Two
The Perfect Storm

When he opened the seventh seal, there was silence in heaven for about half an hour. And I saw the seven angels who stand before God, and seven trumpets were given to them. Another angel, who had a golden censer, came and stood at the altar. He was given much incense to offer, with the prayers of all God's people, on the golden altar in front of the throne. The smoke of the incense, together with the prayers of God's people, went up before God from the angel's hand. Then the angel took the censer, filled it with fire from the altar, and hurled it on the earth; and there came peals of thunder, rumblings, flashes of lightning and an earthquake. Revelation 8:1-6 (KJV)

What powerful imagery the Scriptures paint in this cosmic event as recorded by the writer of the book of Revelation. Thunder, lightning and earthquakes seem somewhat paradoxical in light of the desperation for answered prayer. It would appear the last thing you need when caught between a rock and hard place is rain, thunder, lightning and earthquakes.

Nevertheless, into every life a little rain must fall. I'm not sure who coined that phrase, but for some reason rainy days are often viewed as somewhat negative. Perhaps, there *is* something melancholic about a rainy day. For some it evokes emotions of depression and that rainy-days-and-Mondays-always-get-me-down feeling.

As I write, the clouds outside my window have gathered in their multifarious forms to bring yet another rainy Monday morning. Instead of creating melancholic emotions and feelings of solitude they have evoked the rumblings and shakings of thunder and lightning not only in the skies, but also deep within my spirit. I see and hear the thunder signaling greatness is just ahead! There is something shifting in the atmosphere and a definite stirring within our small planet. Hurricanes are sweeping through regions that have never experienced flooding, wreaking havoc and mayhem along their paths. The weathercaster announced that the largest hurricane in the history of the Pacific is brewing even now! The perfect storm!

When I began writing this book, it seemed as though it had rained for forty days and forty nights because we endured a deluge of rain for over a month. Now, a couple of years later, the earth has suffered tsunamis, earthquakes, flooding and atmospheric pressure like never before, and the flooding continues. On the east coast, they have reported 20 people dead due to flash floods. The earth is yearning for a manifestation of the sons of God!

As I pen this portion of my book, I am in remembrance of the many fatalities and thousands of homes that were destroyed by what was called a "frankenstorm". Hurricane Sandy ripped across the Jersey shore and left many homeless with damages in excess of billions of dollars.

The perfect storm takes on different definitions according to each individual. Being in perfect alignment with God's perfect will and knowing and recognizing the signs that a storm is approaching will forewarn us that impending danger is just ahead. Sometimes, deep within our subconscious mind, we already know that the choice we made was not good. That is Holy Spirit nudging us, letting us know that a storm is just ahead, often due to our own choices and not some demonic attack.

Many war-torn countries are experiencing storms of epic proportions and experiencing economic collapses with no lifelines in sight. Trust me; I am not trying to paint the worst-case scenario as an antithesis so I can then provide a thesis or answer. I am not creating a problem and then, coming in like a hero with the solution! The world is in the midst of a storm. There are "wars and rumors of wars…" We are living in *"those"* days, and it's time we learned how to effectively pray! "Why sit we here till we die?" Let's do something about our situation! Now, before you argue that you already know how to pray, and your morning and evening rituals consist of a time for prayer – hear me out. It is not *"what"* you pray that is most important; it's *"how"* you pray. The *"what"* is irrelevant since God already knows what we pray. It is the *"how"* that Jesus focused on with His disciples. He taught them *how* to pray. Because *how* has to do with the motive behind the prayer.

If ever there was a time and need for a perfect prayer, it is now! The economic world has been teetering on the brink of total decimation for some time now, and many believe that a brooding, perfect storm is ready to pounce and already peering over the horizon.

Prayer is much more than mere words and formulaic methods established by man. God looks for the intent of each cry. Motive, faith, trust, and more trust are the true ingredients for the perfect prayer. Can one ever truly be certain that the motive of prayer is absolutely in right standing with God's perfect will to accomplish what is requested? Is there a proven method to reaching God and accessing the vault of heaven for one's desperate needs? Desperation is a very familiar word to anyone facing hardship. Desperation often plays a large role in the alignment for God's will to be carried out. In the Scriptures, a woman by the name of Hannah cried out to God for a child, and her cries were heard, and a miracle birth was granted. Still, there are many factors hidden within this isolated instant where God responded to someone's cry. Think of the many times you may have cried out in desperation only to feel as though the heavens were shut up and made of brass.

Perhaps, you are thinking to yourself that I am enamored with the word "perfect", and you may be thinking there is no such thing as perfection in this life. When it comes to you and me, naturally, there is no such thing. However, dealing with a perfect God, you must understand that His ways are without flaw. The perfect prayer will lead you to the perfect will of God, and the perfect will of God will lead you into the very presence of a loving Father who desires worship, thus leading one to believe that the motive for prayer should be more of a worshipful plea than a request.

A little rain in the midst of your perfect day could very well be the source for your greatest encounter with the Almighty. With that in mind, may the rains of God's mercy fall and water the seed of desire within each of your prayers. Prepare for the harvest!

Throughout the years, perhaps even centuries, there has been a vast array of books written on the topic of prayer. Many prolific writers have penned their insights, revelations and understanding on the subject. Yet, it seems there is always something missing in these formulas because if the answer to prayer is not always a yes, there is no formula to explain why. Perhaps, the rote formulas prove a hit and miss approach more than an accurate, precise aim.

In the book of Matthew, Christ takes his disciples onto the side of a mountain and begins teaching them *how* to pray. Did you catch that? Let me reiterate, that it is not "*what*" you pray, rather "*how*" you pray. I can only imagine what these men, who had undoubtedly prayed many prayers in synagogues and temples must have thought when Christ said, "Your prayers are all wrong, pray in this manner." You too may be thinking, "What's wrong with the way I pray?" It is evident that Christ had a specific formula in mind for prayer that did not fit the normal methodology of the day. His perfectly executed model prayer known as The Paternoster, The Our Father, or the LORD'S Prayer is probably the best known agreeable factor among Evangelical Christians of every persuasion. This prayer is the one common denominator when navigating through the plethora of denominations from Catholicism to Charismatic/Full Gospel circles. This all-encompassing prayer is more than a model prayer; rather, it *is* the only prayer! The words that Christ taught the disciples were an excerpt of a traditional Jewish prayer. Christ did not come up with a "new" prayer; instead, he took the ancient words and made them flesh, He made them relevant.

Growing up, I was privileged to have Dr. Larry Lea as my youth pastor and close friend. He wrote a powerful book on the LORD'S Prayer that catapulted his ministry into a global success. I am convinced that simply giving honor to prayer unlocks a power of increase and wealth that few know is available. God is a rewarder of them that diligently seek him. One of my other ministry friends, Dr. Juanita Bynum, was teaching on the topic of prayer in London, England, where we both shared the same stage before 15,000 hungry souls waiting to hear a message from God. Juanita had some powerful commentaries about the purpose of going behind the veil. She carefully wove together passages that gave credibility to the idea that the purpose of gaining access behind the veil was to make intercession and petition for others' needs. Still, I see many within the Kingdom who have not experienced equal success employing these formulas. Can it be that there is yet a missing element or link? I am by no means discrediting what my colleagues have written. I am simply building on the foundation of their revelations.

You can access every human need through The Perfect Prayer because it is not about eloquence of speech; rather, it is about alignment with God's perfect will. You will see that prayer really does nothing to move God because God is immovable. Instead, prayer aligns the one praying physically, emotionally, spiritually and mentally for the manifestation of the answer, which is sent the moment you pray. The reason some prayers, seemingly, go unanswered is directly related to the misalignment in the person and not in God's will or desire to answer. Everything you will ever need already exists; you simply have not aligned yourself to bring it to fruition. 2 Peter 1:3 (KJV) According as his divine power hath given unto us all things that pertain unto life and godliness… Everything you need is within reach and already belongs to you!

Christ ascended into the heavenlies and forever sits at the right hand of the Father making intercession for the people of God. That means every request you and I could ever make will never out-weigh the petitions made by our great intercessor, Christ. Historically, prayer has always been viewed as a last ditch effort instead of the quintessential format for accessing the will of God. If Christ's sole purpose is to be seated at the right hand of the Father to make intercessional pleas for His people, what then, is the use for prayer? If the Father already knows every need long before it ever leaves our lips, what then, is the purpose of prayer? If God is sovereign and works in accordance with His own will, what then is the criterion for answered prayer? Could it be that we have reached a level of maturity as the Body of Christ where we must admit that change is inevitable? If some prayers are answered and some are not, does it not merit a deeper inquiry into the power of answered prayer? I think we both agree that our prayers have become more powerful, verbose, eloquent, direct, poignant, effectual, and fervent; and yet, requests often, still go unanswered. We stand back scratching our heads and then head back into our prayer closets and war rooms hoping, this time, it will work. The Scriptures are filled with history-making prayers. I am ready for my prayers to make history; aren't you?

CHAPTER THREE
THE HISTORY OF PRAYER

When I was about nine years old, I attended my first symphony. I remember being overwhelmed by the beautiful auditorium with its finely appointed details and accoutrements. The orchestra pit began to rise and I saw violinists, cellists, French horn players, timpani players, clarinetists, and so many other players preparing. In that instance, the glistening of the chimes drew my eyes, and I saw bows bobbing up and down every which way, I knew I was in for something great! I remember thinking, if this is the opening act and mere warm-up, the full symphony must be heaven on Earth! The lights went dim; a spot shown brightly center stage. A man in a black tuxedo slowly, methodically and determinately takes his place behind the podium. Suddenly, all preparations and movements of the players cease, and every eye is on the conductor. He takes the small baton in his hand and raises both arms and every musician on the stage, simultaneously raised their bows, woodwind instruments, horns, drumsticks, mallets; and then, the Maestro brings the music to life with the slightest movement of his hands and arms. My skin began to tighten as goose bumps covered my arms, legs,

11

chest and neck. Even my scalp crawled. I was captivated, entranced, enchanted and hooked on classical music forever!

The idea that a group of diverse people could be brought together by one common denominator to create masterful sounds was more than my nine year old mind could grasp. People connected to each other by the simple medium of music could only achieve such mastery through the concerted efforts of everyone involved. The music swelled and embedded visions in my mind. Sometimes, when I am quiet and tranquil, I can still hear the notes. Deep inside my being, I can see the notes dancing, bobbing up and down. Music created an indelible mark in my life, and it is these same notes that produced the musician I am today. I can sing, play the piano, write music, and more importantly, I can hear the songs of the Spirit.

Now, I understand why the building that housed this heavenly, symphonic music had to be appointed with beauty and opulence. It was more than simply drawing a captive audience to appreciate the music; the music needed a well-adorned place to facilitate the glory of its fullness.

Prayer is much like a symphony. Many musicians participate in bringing to fruition what already exists in the heart and mind of the maestro, and each musician must follow the Maestro's direction. The great Maestro of life's symphony is the One Who orchestrated all that exists and continues to direct those who will follow His path, His will and His ways – those who will become His instruments of music.

The great Maestro has some preconceived ideals for each of the players. God says, Jeremiah 29:11 (KJV) For I know the thoughts that I think toward you…

The music of your life is playing out whether you like it or not. You must decide whether you will play the song of the Spirit or the song of self.

All too often, people weigh their spirits down by the burdens, petitions and sorrows of the ones for whom they intercede. Perchance, the Maestro never intended for anyone to play the song that was already played by the one born to bear our burdens. I trust you will glean something from this book that will lead you into a balanced and blessed prayer life with no sorrow added.

Throughout history, prayers have had a great effect in shaping man's spiritual quest. The Old Testament records numerous prayers counted worthy of being recorded in the annals of time. We find both common and extraordinary words immortalized by the power of writ in accordance with the courts of the LORD. Some prayers took on poetic and verbose forms while others soliloquized a heartfelt, earnest request that oftentimes, went unmet. Amidst this spiritual inquest, man has always desired to know the reasons behind answered and unanswered prayer.

Prayer is so much more than petition; it is the alignment of body, mind, and spirit with Holy Spirit and the perfect will of the Father. Praying without ceasing is more about walking in the realm of the divine while remaining in alignment with Holy Spirit. It is walking in integrity — the integrity of Holy Spirit and not the good works of man.

We often refer to someone as a person of integrity because of their honesty, but it is not until their thoughts and heart are completely aligned with their actions that they are truly walking in integrity. A person may do one thing in their actions, but their heart is not in it, and therefore, it is not backed by true integrity.

God has equipped each believer with faith, hope, expectancy and a sure confidence. Hebrews 10:35 (KJV) Cast not away therefore your confidence, which hath great recompense of reward. To reach the reward, one must be willing to follow the directions of the conductor. No symphony ever conducted itself. Any attempts at performing without the conductor would lead to a cacophonous mélange of unappreciated, undervalued music. Greatness comes to those who surrender to the power of the conductor's direction. Talk show host, Oprah Winfrey, said something to the effect that surrendering does not mean giving up; instead, it is yielding to the backup system of God's help. Yielding and surrendering to the backup system of God's help gives birth to a deep spiritual confidence that can only come from God. The more you know, the more confident you become.

WISDOM PRINCIPLE: INFORMATION IS THE BIRTHPLACE OF CONFIDENCE.

All things work together under divine direction. When we follow the directives, confidence paves the way to manifestation. Manifestation is the expected optimal response to prayer. Who has ever prayed a prayer expecting nothing? And yet, expectancy is not the sole ingredient to answered prayer. If necessity, desperation and expectancy were the catalyst to answered prayer, God would respond to every child crying out in desperation for protection from an abusive parent. There is a reason I Corinthians 13 says, "Now abideth faith, hope, and love"… because you cannot have love without believing and hoping for something better.

God has given mankind the gift of faith. Faith plays its foundational notes in the symphony of life much like the rhythm sections of an orchestra. Hope is like the gentle, refined descant notes of the flute or the piccolo. Their notes dance around the soft, quiet, and sometimes, subtle sounds of the violins. Faith, then, forges the way for hope, and hope signals the way for something fresh and new creating an expectancy of the next virtuoso written in the score by the creator of the music. Expectancy sounds the alarm that something unknown is just ahead. A moment later, when one thinks the music has taken on a familiar pattern; the trumpets, coronets, and trombones herald the entrance of the spectacular! The timpani rumble reverberating their low tone frequencies from the floor to the walls announcing the coming finale. With each crescendo and clashing of the cymbals, the vision of the music comes to fruition and closes out with the power of faith, letting you know that what you have heard is real. Ah, manifestation! The final component is confidence in what you have believed. Hebrews tells us to hold on to our confidence because it has a great recompense of reward. There is a reward in holding on to certain patterns, prayers and rituals. Just as the orchestra reads from a scripted musical score that may have been penned centuries ago and creates music that can move and motivate the listener, a prayer can do the same.

The Perfect Prayer holds something important that God desires for us to understand. Enfolded in this prayer is something invaluable and of great importance if God saw fit for it to be set apart within Scripture. There are a few recorded prayers in the Bible with a clear reason and purpose. Oftentimes, people stray from rote, ritualistic prayers, thinking it is nothing more than vain repetition; when all the while, it is what God desires regardless of its apparent redundancy.

In many churches, we hear rote prayers recited without a full comprehension of content, intent or desired end. Every prayer has an original intent, and an original meaning that only the person praying knows because the one uttering the prayer is the one who spoke the word and gave birth to the vision encapsulated within the words of their prayer. Jesus/Yahshua prayed The LORD'S Prayer thousands of years ago, but his intent has never changed, and Scripture supports that God's Word is forever settled in heaven. Therefore, it is important to know the true meaning and intent of a prayer.

It is easy to miss unarticulated patterns in this prayer; however, these patterns were clear and concise within the heart of the one who prayed the prayer initially. When Jesus/Yahshua prayed this prayer, his true intentions were made known regardless of whether the disciples understood what he was trying to teach them. **The intent of a prayer is stronger than even the words articulated.** The English translation of the prayer from its original Aramaic language goes like this:

> *Our heavenly father, hallowed is Your name.*
> *Your kingdom is come.*
> *Your will is done, as in heaven so also on earth.*
> *Give us the bread of our daily needs,*
> *and leave us serene,*
> *just as we also allowed others serenity*
> *and do not pass us through trial, except separate us*
> *from the evil one.*
> *For yours is the kingdom, the power, and the glory,*
> *to the end of the universe of all the universes. Amen.*

Allow me to dissect the first three lines of the prayer for a clearer understanding, making it easier to grasp and perceive. In the popularized King James Version, the prayer opens with a declaration of where God's supposed dwelling place should be, while the Aramaic declares Him the "heavenly" Father. You must have a perception of God as being greater than a "Being" who just lives in heaven, and a God who is heavenly. The traditional prayer, then, assumes a position of man having the power to "hallow" His name. Hallowed "*is*" your name... We do not have the power to make anything holy or hallowed. Instead, it is a decree of what already is; His name *is* holy! Whether man regards it holy or not, it remains indubitably holy.

15

Hallowed is your name, your kingdom is come, your will is done... Three emphatic statements establish the foundation for the Perfect Prayer. In Christ's model prayer, the first few words of dialogue leave no room for requests. And yet, prayer has always been about cutting to the chase and making a request to the LORD. "Let's pray. Heavenly father, we need this, we need that. Please give us this and do this for us *now...*"

There are seven parts to this holy prayer. In the first portion of the prayer, we find three parts concerning the glory of God. *Our heavenly father, hallowed is your name. Your kingdom is come...* Jesus/Yahshua told his disciples, "the kingdom of God is within you." This establishes the Kingdom and therefore is not something we pray *will* come. *Your will is done, as in heaven so also on earth.* In other words, YAHVEH'S will is complete not only in heaven, but in all the Earth as well. This leaves no room for a clashing of wills; instead, it reveals a charted, predestined path. I do not claim to hold the answers to deep theological debate concerning predestination; however, I am certain that there is a righteous path that leads to the fulfillment of all of God's promises for each one of us. That is what The Perfect Prayer does; it leads you to that predestined, righteous path where everything you ever wanted and need already exists.

There is something you must understand about the will of God. In His presence, there is no other will allowed or permitted. To approach the throne room of grace with your own will in tow is precisely why God has covered His throne-room with grace. I will explain the four remaining points of the LORD'S Prayer further along in this chapter.

I believe all answered prayer is in accordance with God's will and the culmination of several key factors, which will be discussed throughout the book. When prayer is answered, it is proof that these key factors have become aligned with God's perfect will. While faith plays a crucial role in answered prayer, it is not the sole foundation for answered prayer as we have come to understand. There are many people filled with faith who pray and never receive answers. Some faith teachings substantiate that faith is the only thing needed for effective prayer. However, God is sovereign and His Word tells us He blesses whom He chooses to bless and therefore, places faith in a different role many are prone to believe. When faith takes its place as the foundation for believing that God is who He says He is, instead of the enforcing power behind your words to produce something you want, faith becomes God's will in action. Our faith does not have the power to move God to action. The power is knowing that He is the God who can activate the words of your prayer to provide the solution. Once your faith finds its proper placement in the protocol of prayer, manifestation is just a whisper away. Answer to prayer is based upon God's ability not the amount of faith one may or may not have. *All* things are possible to them that believe!

Another consideration is timing: when you pray...when you petition...when you ask for what you ask...you must not pray *into* the future; you must pray in the NOW. God's name is *always* holy; His kingdom *always* comes, and His will is *always* done. This gives new understanding and enlightenment to the passage found in the book of Hebrews: *Now*, faith is the substance of things hoped for, the evidence of things not seen. Most prayers are offered expecting an answer in the future instead of in the now. When you pray, believe that His will is already done in the matter for which you are praying.

Notice that this translation of The Perfect Prayer ends with a connection that goes beyond forever and ever, as in the traditional LORD'S Prayer. To say, "... *to the end of the universe of all universes"* implies that there are multiple time zones. God's timing or time zone is timeless. He is not limited to the ticking of time like that of our universe. He is from everlasting to everlasting, the Ancient of Days, the Ageless-timeless One. In Him, there is no time. He is NOW; He is forever!

Scientifically, it is understood that events that have already happened in Earth's stratosphere have yet to happen in the outer regions of the universe or the heavenlies. The energy or frequencies of past or present events have not reached those galaxies yet. This is why Scripture admonishes the believer to believe the report of the LORD. Because the LORD'S report is already done and is always a better outcome than what we desire. God's report is based on happenings in the heavenlies not on what's happening here on earth. Are you beginning to see from the perspective of God's view? You may be praying for something that has not yet happened in the realms and dimensions of the heavenlies beyond your reach. This is why Scripture teaches us to bind whatever is *already* bound in heaven and loose whatever is *already* loosed in heaven. Matthew

18:18 (ISV) I tell all of you with certainty, whatever you prohibit on earth will have been prohibited in heaven, and whatever you permit on earth will have been permitted in heaven.

If a meteorite heading towards earth destroyed all of mankind, astronauts flying into outer space could actually watch it happen after it already happened because of the vast difference in time zones between here and there. What am I saying? What you think may have already happened to destroy your life or the lives of people you love may not have happened where God is concerned or where He dwells. The *God perspective* is always different than man's perspective. That is why He can undo what is in our realm, because in His realm or Kingdom, it may not have happened yet. And this is why we can call those things, which be not as though they were because they already happened in His atmosphere. My spirit rejoices within me when I consider this revelation. I want to begin seeing everything from the God perspective because that means anything is possible.

There are many prayers that have been popularized over the centuries that were prayed by simple and humble people. These prayers still minister to many of us hundreds and even thousands of years later. That's the God perspective!

THE PRAYER OF ST. FRANCIS

The prayer of St. Francis of Assisi has for years been a source of encouragement and peace for many. Of course, this prayer has appealed more to those with a persuasion towards Catholicism. Still, in many charismatic circles, this prayer is often used as lovely lyrics for songs of worship. And why not, when such a noble and humble request is made to the Almighty to make of us an instrument of peace and worship, what could be better?

THE PRAYER OF SERENITY

Let us not forget the prayer that has helped countless of millions who have battled with different forms of addiction. "God grant me the serenity to accept the things I cannot change, the courage to change the things I can and the wisdom to know the difference." Perhaps, more than just people with addictive behaviors could benefit from this request.

THE PRAYER OF JABEZ

The recent phenomenon of this simplistic prayer was published in a small book that took the country by storm. The prayer of Jabez opened up an avenue for tapping into the power of words spoken long ago. It was as though the modern contemporary writer had uncovered a magical combination of words that promised to bring prosperity and increase into the life of the one praying. It sold millions of copies and some experienced prosperity and increase; however, not all who prayed the prayer experienced the same. Not to say there was no real benefit from this prayer, but not all who recited the prayer realized a gain. Nevertheless, prayer has been more of a hit or miss action, leaving many wondering what they did wrong or, perhaps, what caused their faith to fail.

In the following chapters, I will explain many misconceptions and expose many anomalies in the art of praying. As you read, you will begin to see and understand the true purpose of prayer and ultimately discover The Perfect Prayer. Isn't everyone searching for the perfect prayer, the prayer that yields the greatest benefits anyway? You might be thinking there is no such thing as a perfect prayer. If you open your mind to a deeper understanding of the supernatural principles of God, you will quickly recognize that there is indeed a deeper understanding to prayer than just blurting out a need or a wish.

Many believers have been brought up being taught to have a strong prayer life, which is more in line with learning how to develop a strong ability to convey needs to God with little teaching about consulting God for what is best. I have come to understand that a prayer life is just that, a "life of prayer." I believe actions, intentions of the heart, and choices are among the many facets of a strong life of prayer. In other words, live your life as a continual prayer: a continual alignment with God's perfect will. I want everything I do, every action I make, to be in constant alignment with Holy Spirit.

Ephesians 1:11 (AMP) In Him we also were made [God's] heritage (portion) *and* we obtained an inheritance; for we had been foreordained (chosen and appointed beforehand) in accordance with His purpose, Who works out everything in agreement with the counsel *and* design of *His* [own] will...

The idea of developing a strong prayer life by cultivating an ability to articulate our needs and the needs of others is simply not compatible with Scripture. God works out everything in agreement with the design of *His* own will. He has already purposed His own will; therefore, we really have no need to articulate our needs. Speaking, praying, begging for our needs does not move God; instead, it helps us recognize our weaknesses and our dependence upon God's response to our prayer.

No prayer has known greater popularity than the familiar, ever miss-understood prayer that we commonly know as the LORD'S Prayer. It is recited in churches, cathedrals, abbeys, and worship centers all over the world. It is the obvious and favored prayer for weddings, funerals, baby dedications, birthday parties and various other festivals and celebrations. It is usually the last ditch effort at making contact with the spiritual dimension for many who are on the edge of death or destruction. The only differing factor across the varied denominations and religions has been the part about "forgive us our debts, or forgive us our trespasses." We will explore this deeper later in this chapter.

Have you ever wondered why some prayers are answered and some are not? You may be wondering if a perfect prayer really does exist; yet, hope somehow drew you to this book, perhaps through its very title. The perfect prayer has nothing to do with who prays it, who believes in it, or the importance of the need. The perfect prayer is a combination, for lack of a better explanation, of supernatural words that can be uttered, virtually, by anyone in the hopes that the vaults of heaven will be opened to reveal the perfect answer.

John Wesley once said, "God does nothing, but in answer to prayer." The question is which prayer? Someone has said that prayers never prayed are prayers never answered. Yet, many prayers prayed with earnest hearts have gone unanswered. My dear friend and colleague, Dr. Myles Munroe, confirmed something I believe to be foundational to the understanding of the components of prayer. (I was heartbroken when I learned of the terrible plane crash on November 9th 2014 that caused the death of he and his beautiful wife and their crewmembers.) He wrote in his book, Understanding the Purpose and Power of Prayer, "Every action taken by God in the earth realm required the involvement of a human being." That is a profound statement that few have ever contemplated. God is bound by the very laws that He established from the beginning of time, ergo, the importance and understanding of prayer. God uses people to carry out His will, His plans, His miracles and every sign and wonder.

WISDOM PRINCIPLE: PRAYER IS THE VEHICLE USED BY GOD'S LAWS TO CARRY OUT HIS WILL ON EARTH.

WISDOM PRINCIPLE: PRAYER IS SIMPLY THE ACKNOWLEDGMENT AND ACCEPTANCE OF THE PERFECT WILL OF GOD.

For years, people have made their habitual treks into various supernatural realms in hopes of deciphering the future via horoscopes, fortunetellers, philosophy, metaphysics and many other mediums. I believe unanswered prayer plays a large role in the apostate condition of many believers. There are countless numbers of people who have called upon God for an answer and have been met with absolute silence. Their unanswered prayer has caused their faith to be conditioned to a level of doubt that supersedes their very faith in God.

Holiness is a key factor in answered prayer because it deals with the right and wrong motive of the individual's heart. When I say holiness, I do not mean holiness as it has been taught for centuries. Holiness is a spiritual attribute, not a physical outward standard. It is a spiritual component of mankind that can only be accessed by Holy Spirit. I am referring to the holiness of Holy Spirit, not religious, legalistic holiness. Holy Spirit is not and has never been a physical entity, and therefore, the holiness of Holy Spirit must be a supernatural attribute. Many believers are steeped in the traditional thinking that holiness is about how you dress or how long you pray. They believe it is tied into restrictions and limitations, like not drinking, cussing or for some even wearing makeup. The holiness that a believer can embody is not based on whether or not he/she does not cuss, spit, chew, sleep around, smoke or drink. The amount of access given to the Holy Ghost by an individual is the sole component that gauges how holy one can be. And Scripture gives no indication that the Spirit is given in doses; rather, we are to be filled with the Holy Ghost. If you are filled with the Holy Ghost, there is no room for demons or devils. According to Strong's Concordance, the word "filled" means: to fill to the top: so that nothing shall be wanting to full measure, fill to the brim. Holiness is the level of righteousness one can achieve not based on works, but rather by the integration of the natural with the supernatural. Holy means "one" as complete or integrated. Holiness is about an integration of body, mind and spirit.

The oneness or integration of holiness stems from the principle of agreement among the Godhead. We find integration in the Godhead or Holy Trinity based on their unending agreement with each other. The proof of agreement is holiness or oneness. The word "integrity" comes from the same root word—integrate. The integrity of a person's heart creates the atmosphere of holiness for answered prayer. My first book entitled *The Agreement: Unlocking The Favor of God* is a powerful revelatory study on the most ancient of God's ordinances: the agreement. We live in a divorced riddled society and few understand the power of staying in the agreement with divine connections. When God wants to bless you, He sends a right person in your life. When evil wants to distract you from your purpose, a wrong person enters your life. *The Agreement* is all about holding on to relationships that hold the answers to healings, blessings, promotions, and many other requests we have made to God. The more agreeable you are, the more favor you will see coming your way!

WISDOM PRINCIPLE: THE FRUIT OF AGREEMENT IS FAVOR.

WISDOM PRINCIPLE: AGREEMENT IS LAYING DOWN ONE'S DREAMS AND EMBRACING THE DREAMS OF ANOTHER.

Agreement is about being at the right place, with the right person, at the right time, every time.

God is a God of integrity because He does what He says. With that in mind, we must understand that effective prayer has nothing to do with eloquence of speech or even desperation! The

Word says, "The effectual, fervent prayer of a righteous man…" Effective prayer is essentially praying what God has already placed or staked His integrity upon, which can only be His own Word and His own perfect will. In the LORD'S Prayer, this is described in the part that says, "as in heaven, so also on earth." Whatever is already bound in heaven can be bound on earth, and whatever is already loosed in heaven can be loosed on earth. Contrary to teaching on the subject of binding and loosing, nothing can be bound or loosed unless it has already been bound or loosed in heaven before hand.

I often wonder how realistic it is to think that inherently evil human beings can actually attain any true integrity. Perhaps, it is more of a process that culminates with God working in and through His perfect will that leads to true integrity. Since integrity is the desired destiny, then, sincerity must be the vehicle that gets us to integration with the will of God.

In the days of the famous sculptors, the Spanish had a saying to validate their work as being without flaw. They would use the term "cin-cera", which means without wax. Some of the sculptors of the day would dishonestly hide the flaws in their marble statues by inserting wax in the flawed cracks and crevices, ergo, "without wax" meant that there were no flaws in their work.

I am convinced sincerity plays a crucial role in prayer. The only way to pray effectively, as mentioned earlier, is to move into the heavenly mindset of the Godhead. The sincerity of your prayer is connected to the integrity of God.

It is Monday morning, and I am still glowing from the effects of the move of Holy Spirit in our Sunday service the day before. I was teaching on the power of the Jewish prayer shawl. We are in the middle of one of the biggest Jewish feasts of the year, and I was encouraging the people to be sure their tithes and offerings were paid up. Not because God needs our money, but because we need God's blessing, increase and protection over our families. I shared with them that Holy Spirit had instructed me to create a tabernacle with my prayer shawl where I, as the priest of the house, could stand under and come into agreement with those who had a need. Except, I made it very clear that if their tithes or offerings were not paid, it would be a waste of time because it would be an *insincere* prayer. Just about everyone in the church came forward, but I was disheartened because some could not come forward because they have been robbing God all year. God has been so gracious to all of them and blessed them in abundance, and yet, they choose to keep one dollar out of ten dollars, a dime out of a dollar. This is blatant thievery, according to Malachi 3:8 (KJV), which states, "Will a man rob God? Yet ye have robbed me. But ye say, 'Wherein have we robbed thee?' in tithes and offerings." Sometimes you have to do something in the natural to unlock something in the supernatural. The tithes and offerings principle may appear as simply being a natural thing, and not a supernatural act, but it is deeply rooted in the culture of Judaism and Christianity. I will expound more on the power of the tithe in a later chapter. Nevertheless, God is always testing the motives of our hearts. In fact, He puts His integrity on the line and allows us to "prove" Him or test Him. This is the only place in the Scriptures that God says, "Prove me…"

How can we know when our motives are wrong or right? How can you know that what you are praying is actually God's perfect will? I do not claim to know everything there is to know about prayer. However, one thing I do know, God always responds to worship.

When your prayer takes on the form of worship, it is connected to an honest, heartfelt plea. Your worship is the integrity of your heart. Worship reveals what is in the deepest part of an individual. It is like shining a light into a prism that refracts light and reflects back toward you illuminating the intent of your heart. Worship makes a critical trajectory journey from the heart through the lips, into the atmosphere, to the throne room of God, and it reflects back revealing the truest intent of one's heart.

WISDOM PRINCIPLE: GOD DOES NOT ALWAYS ANSWER PRAYER, BUT HE ALWAYS RESPONDS TO WORSHIP.

I have had people argue this point with me because they believe that God always answers prayer with a yes, a no, a maybe or later. I understand this concept; however, how many times have you prayed and literally got no answer? There have been times when I prayed and felt like I wasn't reaching God or that He could not hear me. Could it be that when we feel like there is no answer the intent of our hearts is not pure? Nevertheless, I have never opened my mouth in worship, whether through music or verse that God did not always respond. I have always felt His presence near when I worship through song.

In other words, worship must precede prayer when aligning your heart with God's will. What is it about worship that moves God? Worship is the act of paying homage from the heart to something or someone revered. If your heart is not right, then, your worship and prayers are not right. When your prayer becomes worship, it moves from petition to thanksgiving: gratitude for the things God has already performed in your life because of His unending mercy and grace. Everything will go back to what is in your heart. Six out of the seven churches mentioned in the book of Revelation had huge ministries and large buildings and were changing their worlds, but God said, "You have lost your first love." The intent of the heart changes when prayer is simply a mode for acquisition and not worship.

I wrote a worship song that describes a thankful attitude even when feeling confounded:

When I don't know what to say.
When I don't know what to do.
I fix my gaze on You.
Because You're beautiful,
You're so beautiful,
And You're perfect in all Your ways.
You're so beautiful, You're so beautiful
You're the Ancient of Days.
When I don't know what to say,
When I don't know what to do,
I fix my gaze on You.

When prayer becomes desperation, a cry, a plea, it moves from request to an open, clear slate where you are ready to accept whatever God wills. How often have you prayed for something that never came to fruition? Have you ever been told the reason your prayer is not answered is because there is sin in your life, or you do not have enough faith? Why didn't your prayer get answered? Did you run out of faith? Probably. Did you have sin in your life? Most

25

definitely! But how can you be sure that is why your prayer went unanswered? This leads me to believe there is another factor at work behind unanswered prayer. Whatever happens now is not as important as the simple desire for something to just happen. Anything is better than the present. It is at this point that the motive of the praying individual goes from selfish desire to being completely open to God's will. "When I don't know what to say, when I don't know what to do, I fix my gaze on You." Prayer goes from petition to an effectual, fervent request the moment one realizes the only option is based solely upon God's ability and not what one's faith can or cannot produce.

There is a familiar idiom that you may have heard before. You have most likely heard the English translation and probably from a magician. Now, before you become leery or skeptical of what I'm about to share with you, remember it's an idiom, and it actually comes from the Hebrew word, "abra k'adabra," which literally means, "I will create as I speak." That's the power behind the prophets who "called those things which be not, as though they were." We are never more like our great Creator than when we create!

Psalm 54:2 (KJV) Hear my prayer, O God; give ear to the words of my mouth. David wrote these words long before the Messiah came along and began to shed light into the mysteries of the Torah. No doubt, desperation was often David's motive for prayer. You can hear desperation and sometimes utter hopelessness in his prayers, but we know that God heard David's cry. He often found himself pleading and begging God for mercy. He desperately needed God to hear his prayer. Yet, his prayer was often coming only from his mouth and not his heart. David is the iconic example of a flawed human chosen by God; yet, his desperate prayers often went unmet. It was not until David prayed in accordance with God's will that things began to change. David was acquainted with the sins of adultery, murder, lust and whatever else plagued his heart, proving that perfection is not the criteria for answered prayer. David was a man after God's own heart. He was a worshiper!

WISDOM PRINCIPLE: GOD IS NOT LOOKING FOR PERFECTION; HE IS LOOKING FOR PRECISION.

God is looking to see if you can precisely follow His instructions to produce the desired end. Prayer is more about precision than passion. There are many people who passionately pray about matters, but miss the point when it comes to precision.

James 5:15 (KJV) And the prayer of faith shall save the sick and the LORD shall raise him up; and if he have committed sins, they shall be forgiven him. The word prayer in this passage comes from the Greek word "yoo'-khom-ahee", which translates as, middle of a primary verb; to wish; by implication to pray to God: pray, will, wish. I like the idea that the actual translation of "pray" means to make a wish. I have always had a different view and approach with making my requests known to God. I like the idea that a wish is usually granted by a genie if the one making the wish follows the protocol. However, prayer is obviously deeper than the fairy tale genie granting you three wishes. For many, it is easier to think all that has to be done is rub the magic lamp and—Voila! Your prayers and wishes are granted! I am convinced that the protocol of prayer plays a greater role in the fulfillment of requests made to God than most people realize. The book of James says we pray amiss. Perhaps, he meant that sometimes, we hit the mark and other times we don't. The rules of the kingdom are very real and can only be unlocked through the protocol of prayer. We live in an age of information, knowledge, social media, blogging, vlogging, opinions and views. It seems that everyone has their opinion on how things should be, but few want to know what has to be done and what has to change to get to the way things should be.

I wrote a blog this morning for my readers on a networking Internet site much like Facebook and Myspace called Mychurch. It is a site where people of like faith can chat, blog, offer prayers, counsel each other, share opinions, and offer advice. You would think this is a formula for success and answered prayer. It should be a safe haven for well-intended writers like me. However, when you touch on taboo subjects like spiritual authority, protocol, showing honor to pastors and each other, people get down right nasty. In my blog, I shared on the topic of the blessing that is promised according to the book of Deuteronomy 28:2 (KJV) And all these blessings shall come upon thee, and overtake thee, *if* thou shalt hearken unto the voice of the LORD thy God.

A man, notorious for being a troublemaker on the site

commented and stated we are blessed simply by the fact that the old covenant is dead, and we are under a new covenant. That is like saying the Old Testament/Covenant is not Scripture! It would be easy to think that we have just been added to the "bless-me-club" by way of Christ and the New Testament, and now, we have nothing to do, but stand and wait for packages to arrive from heaven without any effort on our part. God always places a prerequisite that must be met before the fulfillment of a promise in Scripture. Both in the New and Old Testaments, every promise has a condition that must be met to unlock the benefit of the promise.

James 5:16 (KJV) Confess your faults one to another, and pray one for another, that ye may be healed. The effectual fervent prayer of a righteous man availeth much.

Notice the protocol: first a confession of sin is made, then, admittance to faults and shortcomings, an eye-to-eye look at one's humanness, and finally, praying for someone else. After this critical journey in the supernatural, prayer reaches a level of efficacy.

Another usage of the word prayer comes from the Greek word, deh'-om-ahee, which means to beg as binding oneself, i.e. petition: beseech, pray (to), make request. The only real request to be made is on behalf of others; then, God moves on the behalf of the petitioner. What you make happen for others, God will make happen for you.

Ephesians 6:8a (KJV) Knowing that whatsoever good thing any man doeth, the same shall he receive of the Lord...

Acceptable prayer has to be sincere, offered with honor and reverential fear. We must pray with a humble sense of our own insignificance in light of the Great I AM, being cognizant of our own unworthiness as sinners, with earnest importunity and with unrelenting submission to *the* divine will.

Adam was not required to pray because God, simply, met all of his needs as he walked with Him in the cool of the day. What does it actually mean to walk with God in the cool of the day? To walk with the Father is to humble yourself and become an agreeable person, a person who is quick to obey God's day-to-day instruction. The most impacting change that took place after man was expelled from the Garden of Eden is the disruption in communication between God and man. After all, God still made provision for Adam and Eve, except that now God expected Adam to call upon Him and declare his need and dependency upon the Great Creator.

I was watching the sitcom, King of Queens, on television, and the episode spoke strongly to my spirit about prayer. I know you're probably thinking, what spirituality is found in a secular show? God is speaking to us through everything around us.

Carrie, one of the main characters in the show, the wife of Doug, the star of the show, reluctantly attends church after having an awkward encounter with the priest of their parish at a grocery store. During the service, Carrie prays for a raise and the next day receives a substantial pay increase. That evening, she assumes her posture for prayer and asks for a pair of Gucci shoes to go on sale. Doug becomes quite upset because he does not feel that she should use prayer for such trivial matters. Of course, the next time Carrie visits the shoe store, her Gucci shoes have been marked down.

Could it be that her simple act of attending the worship service has positioned her for what God already wanted to give her, and all she needed was to align her mind and attitude with God's? Do you believe that God really wants to bless you?

The story continues when Doug finally joins in with Carrie and begins praying for his favorite team to be victorious over their opposing team, and miraculously, they win! Finally, Doug and Carrie find themselves at their local fish market where they run into the parish priest once again. There is one Mahi-Mahi left and the good father has his eye on the coveted fish. Doug prays that God will allow him to have the fish instead of the priest. The man of the cloth miraculously changes his mind midstream and asks for a different kind of fish. Sometime later, Doug and Carrie show up at church, but the priest is out due to food poisoning from the fish he had purchased. Doug feels really bad and decides that this kind of praying lacks integrity because his motives were all wrong.

Often-time believers are much like Doug and Carrie; they pray to get things, but then, as in this sitcom episode, they only serve God when a need arises or something catastrophic happens that requires supernatural assistance. Any time you come under the delusion of self-preservation, you open yourself for disastrous happenings that could ultimately destroy you. There was a time when man did not have the privilege of calling upon the name of the LORD.

Genesis 4:26 (KJV) And to Seth, to him also there was born

a son; and he called his name Enos: *then began men to call upon the name of the LORD.* The name Seth means compensation and has a numeric value of six, which of course is the number of man. Something happened during the course of human events that changed the dynamics of life on earth and caused men to call upon the name of the LORD. Up until this point, there was a different arrangement for communication between God and man. It was not until Enos was born that man began to cry out to God. In the beginning, according to Genesis 4:26, prayer was more of a simplistic and humble cry to God. It was man simply calling upon the name of the LORD/YAHVEH. Perhaps, we would have greater success taking this approach when making requests to God. A child in need simply calls upon one of the parents, who quickly assesses the need and tends to it. A child is not required to make a formal request to the parent except to call out for Mommy or Daddy!

Although primitive men were uncivilized by today's standards and uneducated in spiritual matters, still, there was power in this humble prayer because of the sheer power in the name of the LORD/YAHVEH.

When I first began researching the topic of prayer, I was overwhelmed at how many books, commentaries, theories, and a host of other ideas and ideals about the topic existed. Unfortunately, many times people read something they've never read before, and they misjudge the writer, the interpreter, the translator, the Scribe who trans-scribed it, etc. We often consider those who view things differently than us as heretics. Ignorance and lack of knowledge are the cause of religiosity and traditions of men. We call people who think differently than us heathens, unsaved, new-agers, we even put them in boxes with labels that we have created for them.

The first time prayer is mentioned in the New Testament is in: Matthew 5:44 (KJV) But I say unto you, love your enemies, bless them that curse you, do good to them that hate you, and pray for them which despitefully use you, and persecute you.

I have always wondered how to truly pray for people who have inflicted pain and harbored a deep-rooted offense. I know that words can be uttered from lips, but oftentimes the heart is confused with emotional demands that go beyond our human ability to pray for someone who has hurt us. I believe that praying for others when they have hurt you is really more for preparing your heart for the ministration of Holy Spirit in your life. It is quite absurd to think that God would bless someone who has hurt you solely on the basis of your half-hearted request. So then, to pray or not to pray is the question. We are instructed to love enemies, bless those who curse us, do good to those who hate us and pray for the ones who despitefully use us. This is where the Perfect Prayer comes into play. If you pray the Perfect Prayer over those who hurt you, it does not involve your feelings and emotions, but rather, the power behind the prayer Yahshua/Jesus taught us to pray.

Our Heavenly Father, grant that this person knows you in your heavenly state.
Make your Holy name known unto them.
Grant that they know your kingdom is come and your will is done.
Give them the bread of their daily needs and leave them serene just as they have allowed others serenity.
Do not pass them through trial, but deliver them from the enemy...

Praying for your enemies in this manner removes the emotional barriers and allows God to do with them according to His will. When you create serenity for others, you reap serenity for yourself. What you make happen for others, God makes happen for you. It's the law of sowing and reaping. You reap serenity only when you "also" allow others serenity. You cannot hold grudges and unforgiveness to others and expect to walk in serenity. That poison is in you! It is eating away at your peace and serenity whether you know it or not.

How did God answer prayer in the Old Testament before faith, pre-Messiah and pre-Holy Ghost? This question finds its answer in a very bizarre and foreign custom that involved two dice called the *urim* and the *thummim*. The word urim, pronounced "oorim", means lights: the oracular brilliancy of the figures in the high priests' breastplate. The word thummim, pronounced "toomim", means perfection: an emblem of complete truth. The High Priests carried two oracular devices that had the appearance of dice in a special compartment of their vesture. They were tossed much like dice are tossed today, and God would manipulate the dice to provide an answer from His throne on high. So in essence, prayer was answered through God's *oracular brilliancy and His emblem of truth.*

Prayer is still in a revolutionary process and will someday culminate with simultaneous/instantaneous manifestation the moment you make a request. Because the more we, as the body of Christ, become like Christ, the more we become the Living Word. When you are the Word, you can speak the Word as though it already is. That is, after all, what Yahshua/Jesus did; he was the Word.

CHAPTER FOUR
THE PROTOCOL OF PRAYER

I face your Temple as I worship, giving thanks to you for all your loving-kindness and your faithfulness, for your promises are backed by all the honor of your name. In this passage, there is a definitive visual of the posturing of the psalmist. The posture of worship is assumed as the precursor for giving thanks. Few, in Christendom, understand or are even aware of the protocol of prayer. Most believers pray for what they want, when they want it, never considering God has a perfect design for each of our lives. Psalm 138:2 (TLB)

As Americans, we should be thankful every waking moment. While the rest of the world is in the grips of war, we are enjoying a decent economic recovery in the "home of the brave and land of the free." America is a nation in the midst of building, expanding and growing while other countries are being demolished and destroyed, ravaged by earthquakes and natural disasters. Somewhere a praying mother, a concerned father, is making supplication and touching heaven on behalf of a son or daughter, and as a collective people,

America is spared God's wrath.

The psalmist makes a distinction between God's loving kindness, His faithfulness and His promises. This is the part of God that most Christians rarely encounter. They experience the loving-kindness and the faithfulness, the hand of God, the providence of God, but they seldom experience the full-fledged, covenant agreement of His promises. There is a difference. God is faithful even if you are not! Remember, we are talking about the protocol of prayer: the proper procedure of prayer. The Bible says God's mercies and lovingkindness endure to all generations. His promises, however, are a different story. Not everyone gets the promises because not everyone is willing to go deep enough to get them. Notice that the writer of this psalm is facing a particular direction in a particular posture when giving praise to the Almighty. That sounds like protocol, procedure and order to me.

I wonder how many Christians talk to God from their beds and say, "God, thank you for this day. Ok, love you, bye." I have always said, "Your posture will dictate what you put out." I do not want to sound religious or imply you must do certain gestures when you come into the house of worship, but if God instructs you to make the sign of the cross and genuflect when you enter, you should do it! If He instructs you to go down on your knees or on your face, then, that is the protocol for your prayer life. Regardless of your religious persuasion, you must do as God instructs and not worry about what others around you may say or what they think. God's instruction may not always be logical to us. Ten years ago, it was not logical for me to buy a bigger, more expensive home when I was already heavily in debt. Nevertheless, that is what God instructed, and He has made provision for my household for the past 11 years. Just one act of obedience has unlocked a windfall of blessings, and several years later, they are too numerous to count. Like the prophet Hosea, who received an instruction from God to marry Gomer, a harlot. You don't get any more illogical than that! I would like to write a book someday and call it, When God Tells You To Marry the Harlot. I don't know how many people would get it, but it's about following the instruction with precision even if it seems illogical.

Unfortunately, the problem for most is the requirement part, the follow-the-stinking-directions part. 2 Chronicles 7:14 (KJV) is very clear on the protocol, the posturing, the required state of mind for God to respond and heal our land. "If my people, which are called by my name, shall **humble** themselves, and **pray**, and **seek** my face, and **turn** from their wicked ways; then will I hear from heaven, and will forgive their sin, and will heal their land." The word seek means to crave, to require as a necessity. God's people must get to the place where they crave and require, as a necessity, His face, His countenance! Imagine a couple in love, but they never look at each other's faces, they never gaze into each other's eyes. This kind of intimacy and love requires humility. "If my people – shall humble themselves and pray... Then will I hear from heaven and will heal their land!" God is ready to heal our lands, our countries, our cities, our communities... He's ready to heal our bodies, our minds and our pasts, but we must be willing to follow the protocol.

When was the last time you had an appointment with your doctor for an illness or physical malady? You went at the appointed time; you answered his questions; you sat or lay on his table for the examination, and perhaps it was a bit humbling if the exam called for removing your clothes or worse! Perhaps the exam called for some probing. Either way, you had to submit yourself to his/her protocol, and the result was healing! We cannot expect God to heal our land if we are unwilling to follow the protocol of prayer. Our heavenly Father, hallowed is Your Name. Your kingdom is come, Your will is done...

Just do what God tells you to do. If He tells you to face north, south, east or west, simply do it because unlocking His promises depends on your willingness to obey His instruction. Don't be like one guy on my blog who has probably never experienced God's abundant blessings of increase, simply because he believes that we don't have to "work" for our blessings. I hardly call kneeling, bowing down, standing or prostrating oneself work. It is more of a privilege and an honor than work. When you ask God for a miracle, He will always give you a directive or a simple instruction to follow. The instruction may not always be logical to you; but if you follow the directive, you will receive your miracle. The doctor gives you a prescription with instructions on what you should or should not eat, and when to take the medication. The result is healing or better yet, a miracle!

God gives instructions to unlock His promises. When you are in search of what will unlock the different dimensions of the power of the Word, you will do whatever it takes. Yahshua prayed an uncommon prayer then he asked the disciples to pray after him, "Our heavenly Father..." This was an uncommon, extraordinary prayer for his generation. In a time of Pharisees' and Sadducees' prayers, Yahshua broke right through man's traditions and busted heaven wide open. Yahshua prayed the Perfect Prayer exactly as his Father instructed him because he never did anything except what his Father instructed. The Bible says he was obedient even unto death. I have a few wisdom principles that I have listed in our church bulletin for several months in a row in the hopes that those who are in rebellion would read them. I believe obedience is the key to unlocking the hidden things in God. God is not looking for perfection; He's looking for precision. He's looking for someone He can show Himself mighty through, just as He did through Christ, who was obedient even unto death.

WISDOM PRINCIPLES ON OBEDIENCE:

OBEDIENCE IS NEVER JUST FOR A SEASON!

OBEDIENCE IS THE ATMOSPHERE FOR MIRACLES!

OBEDIENCE IS THE FOUNDATION FOR PROMOTION!

OBEDIENCE IS THE PASSION OF RIGHTEOUSNESS!

OBEDIENCE IS THE FRUIT OF HOLINESS!

OBEDIENCE IS THE AUTHORITY OF THE BELIEVER!

The criterion for answered prayer is simply obedience. That may sound a bit far-fetched; however, allow me to shed light on something supernatural awaiting you if you will just do what God instructs you. You must follow God's instruction quickly because if you allow yourself to ponder the matter, you may talk yourself out of the original instruction. Unlocking the dimensions of the power of

God's Word means you will do whatever God calls for you to do. Are you ready to go to another dimension of God's power? Prepare yourself for a great move of the Holy Ghost; and when I say prepare, I don't mean, "try" to be more spiritual. Instead, align yourself with God's will. Prayer is all about alignment, alignment, alignment. When your spirit, mind and body come into alignment with the perfect will of God, answers to prayers are just a breath away.

Christ understood the importance of aligning himself to the will of his Father and ultimately gained the universe, received his Father's name and was assigned a seat at His right hand. Christ is seated at the right hand of the Father making intercession on our behalf. If Christ is interceding for us, what can we possibly add to the perfection of his prayer? Prayer should be a decree and a command, not a request. Christ did not stop to pray before he healed the hurting; he simply commanded them to be healed because he was aligned with his Father's will.

Perhaps, the notion of decreeing or commanding something to be or not to be goes against your preconceived traditions of prayer. You may even feel as though mankind has no right to use God's Word to make demands of Him. Most Christians are used to begging, instead of walking in authority and decreeing what it is they want. Christ made demands on water, fig trees and many other elements of the earth. Moreover, it is not a command when it was God's idea to begin with. There is simple beauty in the principle I am trying to convey to you. When you pray the perfect will of God, you do not have to ask; you simply decree, command or speak something from the realm of the supernatural into fruition: into the natural.

The authority of a prayer is not based so much on the individual praying, but on the source of the prayer. Prayer is just as much about the verbal content as it is faith. The book of James says, "...and the prayer of faith shall save the sick." This verbiage indicates or at best leads us to believe that there are specific prayers for specific needs. Yet, the title of my book leads you to believe that there is one Perfect Prayer. Exactly! This book will not only open your heart to receive the revelation of The Perfect Prayer, but it will prove itself even before you finish reading. The secret revealed here is that "the prayer of faith" *is* the Perfect Prayer. I am going to pause in the middle of this chapter, and we're going to pray together. And I believe, the prayer of faith shall save the sick. If you are sick, get ready to be healed. If you are bound, get ready to be set free. If you need a financial breakthrough, get ready for the breakthrough! Let's pray together in agreement:

Our heavenly Father,
Hallowed is Your name.
Your kingdom is come, Your will is done,
As in heaven so also on earth.
Give us the bread of our daily needs and leave us serene,
Just as we also allowed others serenity.
And do not pass us through trial.
Except separate us from the evil one.
For Yours is the kingdom, the power and the glory.
To the end of the universe of all universes. Amen.

And the prayer of faith shall save the sick! The whole premise of this prayer is to elevate you above your problems. Most believers go to God in prayer burdened down with their problems, but this prayer will catapult you into a dimension beyond what you may be experiencing in the natural. Instantly, you are taken into the Spirit realm where things that are not real on earth already exist in heaven. But you can only see these things through God's perfect will. Most believers know very little about God's *perfect will.* They know some about His *good will,* and the majority is stuck in His *permissive or acceptable will.*

Romans 12:2 (KJV) And be not conformed to this world: but be ye transformed by the renewing of your mind, that ye may prove what is that good, and acceptable, and perfect, will of God. This is a progression not a choice! You begin with God's *goodness*, and then, you move to the *acceptable* and ultimately to the *perfect* will of God.

His will is already done and positioned to bless you. You simply align yourself to His perfect will.

His will is to heal you.
His will is to prosper you.
His will is to increase you.
His will is to resurrect anything that has died.
His will is to position you for favor.
His will is to give you what you want even before you ask!

38

As a child of God, there is nothing we ask for that we receive that is outside of His will. If God gives it to you, it is because it is a part of His will. He wants you to have the blessed life now!

1 Thessalonians 5:18 In every thing give thanks: for *this* is the will of God in Christ Jesus/Yahshua concerning you. The will of God is found in your attitude of gratitude, not in finding your purpose in life. Many Christians spend half of their lives praying and seeking counsel trying to figure out God's will for their lives, confusing it with their purpose. Your purpose cannot be discovered until you move into God's perfect will. The will of God is connected to something supernatural, not a job, a career, a calling or simply an anointing. The Perfect Prayer will launch you into a dimension beyond searching for an earthly purpose into the supernatural realm where your purpose is revealed. It is a matter of discovering His will first, and then your purpose ensues.

You cannot manipulate God into giving you anything that He has not already predestined for you. It is pivotal to understand the correct and formal approach to the throne of God. I agree that God can hear and can answer the simple prayer of a child or a brand new believer. What I am trying to convey is the importance of recognizing that there comes a time when we must reach a level of maturity where you know how to properly navigate within the kingdom.

Your approach and response to a man of God is part of the proper protocol to prayer. The people who did not receive Yahshua as the Messiah did not receive anything from him. Many came for healing, but only certain people received their miracles. Their faith was in the healing, not the healer. This may sound like God is a respecter of persons. I am not contesting the Scripture that clearly states that God is no respecter of persons. However, could it be that what God allows and accepts as proper protocol for prayer from some, could reveal what He approves or disapproves?

There are seasons God has predestined for each individual. Just as He has every hair on your head numbered, He has planned your seasons and your appointed times. Let me reiterate that I do not believe any kind of prayer can manipulate God to give you anything unless He has already predestined you to receive it. I shared something to this effect on an online church social media site and one person was quick to comment, "Why bother praying?" Prayer is not about convincing God to give us what we want; instead, it helps the one praying to have faith and to trust God. Prayer aligns your mind, thoughts, and your physical body to God's perfect will, which existed before you even prayed! The question then is, how to discover your appointed time with destiny.

Predestination does not mean God has decided everything for us. It means our right choices put us on the path that God has decided is the very best path for each of our lives. Your choices either keep you on or off the path of God's appointed destiny.

The Israelites were the first to establish the foundation of all faith. The foundation of faith is not based on the Apostles, but on the doctrines that had been pre-established by the Israelites who studied Torah. Prior to the Messiah's arrival, the children of Israel had only dealt with the sovereignty of God. This era was pre-grace, pre-Messiah and pre-Holy Ghost. The Israelites believed God would deliver them, but were clueless on the logistics. They could accept that God would deliver them because they believed in His name, which means God of covenant.

The key to answered prayer it to step into the divine will of the sovereign God because He is all-knowing. He knows exactly what you need before you even pray. Therefore, prayer is not about making God aware of what He already knows; rather, its purpose is to convince you and align your will with His. It's like being at the right place at the right time all the time.

Proverbs 3:5 (KJV) In all your ways acknowledge him and he will direct your path. He will align your steps, your path and unfold his master plan for your life. When the Almighty hears you crying out, He is not so much moved by your tears, but rather, by your obedience. The dynamics are now shifted to the fact that you are now broken enough to follow His instructions and protocol, and thus, His will unfolds. It is not so much about speaking the right combination of words, petitions and requests with the perfect amount of faith. It is about bringing yourself into a place where you align with His perfect will, where what He has prepared for you becomes accessible.

Something powerful is unlocked when you pray like Jesus/Yahshua taught. When you pray the Perfect Prayer, you are aligned and connected to the entire Kingdom of Heaven. I promise you, if you don't know anything else to say when you pray, try the Perfect Prayer. You will access something beyond your current dimension, much like what happened at the Pool of Bethesda.

At the Pool of Bethesda, at a certain appointed time of the year, an angel would appear and stir the waters. Timing was everything! The first person to jump into the pool would receive healing. Notice, I said at the appointed time. It was not a random healing; it was on purpose. God does nothing by accident or randomly. Certain elements were set into motion, and then ordered to intersect at the appointed time. When you move into the perfect will of God, you come out of the "accident zone" and into the "incident zone." You are in the zone of the Spirit; you have moved into the zone where the Bible tells us "a thousand will fall at your side and ten thousand at your right hand, but none shall come nigh your dwelling." Now, journey and the path become a little easier to follow. Imagine being surrounded by a thousand on one side and ten thousand on the other, but not a one of those people against you can touch you. That's a supernatural zone of protection!

If you went to the doctor because you were experiencing abdominal pain, would you request that he cut out your kidney to rid you of the problem, or would you allow him to diagnose and treat you accurately in accordance with a conclusive test? When we align ourselves with the perfect will of the Father, we receive an accurate diagnosis and the correct treatment. We are put through a battery of tests to conclude our diagnosis to best treat whatever the problem may be.

It's not the prayer that moves God; but rather, that we have approached Him through the proper, prescribed protocol. Did you follow the instructions? Did you do what He said? Were you at the right place at the right time? Did you jump into the pool before anyone else? Did you dip in the Jordan River seven times?

James 4:3 (AMPC), "...because you ask with wrong purpose and evil, selfish motives. Your intention is [when you get what you desire] to spend it in sensual pleasures." It's like praying for something that has already been provided. Everything that comes to pass in a believer's life is by God's design. Everything God does on earth is subject to the laws He has established from the beginning of time. God will never violate nor contradict His own laws.

Ephesians 6:18 (NKJV)…praying always with all prayer and supplication in the Spirit, being watchful to this end with all perseverance and supplication for all the saints. If we pray "in the Spirit" for someone, we cannot pray focusing on a disease or sickness because in the Spirit, the realm of God's perfect will, disease and sickness do not and cannot exist. In the perfect will of God, these things are nonexistent. Pray instead, in the *now*, and decree that they *were* already healed and focus on the power of God's Word already resident within them as sons of God.

1 Peter 2:24 (KJV) Who his own self bare our sins in his own body on the tree, that we, being dead to sins, should live unto righteousness: by whose stripes ye *were* healed. In due season, in God's timing, your miracle will happen! It has nothing to do with the power of any man; rather, it is the ultimate display of the sovereignty of God, Who has set things into motion to happen in accordance with His Word. Many believers are oblivious to the continuity of God's work all around them. He works all things together for good! They come and go as they please in accordance with their needs, and then, they find themselves in a desert and feel like giving up, and finally acquiesce to the protocol of prayer. They get an answer to their prayer, and they call it a miracle!

Think about the miracles of Christ. When something was out of order, there were times when Jesus/Yahshua could not or would not perform miracles. Christ did not go about dealing with diseases on the surface; he dealt with the inner workings of the individual down to the genetic code. This proves He was aware of the external needs, but based his answer directly in response to the intent of the individual. Our God is not a surface healer; He heals the issue and cause.

Is your faith established enough to believe that God is who He says He is? If you wrap your faith around a house, a car or other things, how can you approach Him and believe Him? This could lead you to a different concept of faith without even knowing it. Many believers unknowingly attempt to manipulate God into giving them what they want, but He is not willing to give you anything until you can align yourself with His Word because He will not violate His own Word. Someone said to me, just this week that the devil answers prayers too. He had prayed for a transfer because he was trying to manipulate a situation where he had prayed for God to restore a relationship with someone who had moved out of state. So, naturally, he thought to pray for a transfer, and he got what he asked for. He counseled with me, and I told him Holy Spirit was showing me that he was missing God if he continued to pursue this person. I told him he was going to move out there, and she was going to end up back in Texas. Thankfully, he listened to my instruction and stayed put. In less than a month, the young lady had relocated back to Texas, just as I had predicted. It's not that the devil answered his prayer; instead, his *willpower* was attempting to override the will of the Father. There are many Christians operating with willpower instead of the power of God's will.

There are probably more prayers offered up referencing healing and the need for physiological miracles than any other need. I believe God can work, not only healing diseases, but He can change your genetic code if need be! That may sound like an impossibility, but that's where God shines! He is the God of impossibilities! I believe God can heal genetic abnormalities. The DNA handcrafted by God for each individual human being is perfect in accordance to God's perfect will, but it is affected by human error that eventually compromises the genetic genome resulting in sickness and disease. Sickness is a disorder, and disorders can only exist outside of the perimeters of a God of perfect order. Many times, Christians think they have to cast out demons, but all that is really needed is to break generational curses that can strap one down genetically.

God knows the exact and precise order of each chromosome, and when you align with His perfect will, everything about you comes into perfect order right down to your chromosomes. However, all it takes is for one chromosome to be out of order to make someone stupid, crazy, lame, dumb, retarded, maimed, blind, deaf, dumb or even evil.

According to God's Word, we understand and it is established that Yahshua referred to himself as the Son of Man, not the Son of God, letting us know that He too is connected to an earthly genetic code or DNA. If he did not have the human genome working in him, he could never have succumbed to death. The book of Ecclesiastes tells us that to everything there is a time (or timeline) and a season. We are all subject to a timeline. The problem is that many of the choices people make cut their timeline short.

Ephesians 3:10-21 (NIV) His intent was that now, through the church, the manifold wisdom of God should be made known to the rulers and authorities in the heavenly realms, according to his eternal purpose that he accomplished in Christ Jesus/Yahshua our Lord. In him and through faith in him we may approach God with freedom and confidence. I ask you, therefore, not to be discouraged because of my sufferings for you, which are your glory. For this reason I kneel before the Father, from whom every family [a] in heaven and on earth derives its name. I pray that out of his glorious riches he may strengthen you with power through his Spirit in your inner being, so that Christ may dwell in your hearts through faith. And I pray that you, being rooted and established in love, may have power, together with all the LORD'S holy people, to grasp how wide and long and high and deep is the love of Christ, and to know this love that surpasses knowledge—that you may be filled to the measure of all the fullness of God. Now to him who is able to do immeasurably more than all we ask or imagine, according to his power that is at work within us, to him be glory in the church and in Christ Jesus/Yahshua throughout all generations, for ever and ever! Amen.

"World without end..." there's a reference to a timeline progressing to timelessness. Paul said something very interesting concerning Christ. Ephesians 3:4 (KJV) Whereby, when ye read, ye may understand my knowledge in the mystery of Christ... Even the Apostle Paul, who lived during the time of Christ and the disciples, had mysteries concerning the Christ.

The whole doctrine of the Christian faith is based on the birth, death and resurrection of Christ. But we must not forget that the Son did nothing without first consulting with the Father and only carried out the will of the Father. And yet, it seems that Christianity has attempted to eclipse the power and authority of the Father. I am convinced this is the reason we are not seeing the miracles and the "mightier works than these" that Jesus/Yahshua said we would do after he ascended. Christian doctrine has created an imbalance in the Godhead that has cost the body of Christ greatly.

Think about the difference in the miracles that took place during the days of the prophets of old and those that occurred when Yahshua walked the earth compared to where we are today. The only difference is that their focus was on the Father. Jesus/Yahshua did nothing unless the Father instructed him. Every miracle was preceded with worship to the Father. The ancient prophets parted the seas, opened blind eyes, and raised the dead before the Savior or the Holy Ghost ever came to earth.

You cannot get where you want to be without following the proper protocol. Yahshua did not have a problem with protocol. He is the way to the Father, and founded on His Jewish roots, he believed and taught that we are to love the LORD our God with all our hearts and all our might. The key motto for the state of Israel is The Shema, "Hear O Israel, the LORD is our God, the LORD is One" (*Shema Yisrael Adonai eloheinu Adonai echad.)* In other words, everyone in the land of Israel recognizes that there is only one God. If you love the Father, you will love everything He has created. Christ himself said, "If you have seen me, you have seen the Father, and if you love me, you love the One who sent me. He said there is One who is greater than I..."

What happens when a son takes on an air of I'm-better-than-my-father? That is rebellion! Yahshua never usurped his position with the Father. He willingly acquiesced to the Father and made it publicly known that he was about the Father's business. He was the Messiah, the anointed one, the chosen one, the appointed one, and he was also flesh with a DNA just like you and me! He needed no help with his deity; he knew who he was because of the Father. He was given the name above all names. He is seated at the right hand of the Father; he was never a manipulator. When something was out of order in the atmosphere, he simply said, "No miracles today!" How did a humble, meek Lamb of God become equal with the Almighty? By submission, by order, by following protocol! He told his own mother when she pressed him to perform miracles that his hour (time) had not yet come. Doesn't anyone question what these things mean? They were not just random happenings in the life of the Messiah.

In the Old Testament, God said His presence would not dwell in the ark and in the temple unless it was built with exact precise measurements according to His instructions. If one thing were out of order, His presence would not dwell among the people. In the building of the temple, even the stones used for the structure were hewn in a different location and brought to the site to avoid chaos, clutter, and disorder. From the inception to construction, the temple was subjected to the protocol of the Father.

God carries out an ongoing conversation in the book of Isaiah regarding His own greatness. He speaks of His power; He declares, "I AM THAT I AM." This is our God defining Himself and telling us who He is. This is neither boasting nor prideful. Pride is not involved when you boast of what is true. Pride is boasting on superficial, external attributes that are temporal.

The traditions of men have made the Word of God ineffective. Why is it that many prophets and evangelists of today can go over to Africa and do mighty exploits, but in America they can barely heal a wart? Maybe because in this country, the protocol required for receiving the mighty move of the Almighty is not respected nor allowed.

Prayer has to be more than just a plea for help. When you follow the proper protocol, you will lock into the perfect will of God. When you lock into the perfect will of God, you will find favor even as you face difficult circumstances. My friend, Dr. Zonnya LaFerney says, "We don't have as many problems, as we have choices to make." When you are locked into the perfect will of God, you will be able to make the right choices that will lead you to the right place at the right time. Timing is everything! You must be in sync with the perfected timing of Holy Spirit.

WISDOM PRINCIPLE: TO BE LOCKED INTO THE PERFECTED TIMING OF THE SPIRIT IS TO WALK IN THE PERFECT WILL OF GOD.

Sometimes, we pray believing that we are not worthy, or we may even feel worthless and fail to recognize that God sees our worth before we even pray. The crucifixion was the point of contact that identified Christ to the name of YAHVEH. It was when his flesh body was crucified that he moved into his glorified body or better yet, he moved into God's absolute, perfect will!

When Mary ran into the Messiah after his resurrection, she

did not recognize him; but when he spoke, she recognized his voice. It was at that moment that mankind had its first glimpse of glory. He instructed Mary not to touch him because he had not yet ascended to the Father.

Something happens when we come into a proper understanding of who God, the Almighty Father truly is. Every encounter with the Son and with Holy Spirit here on Earth is all for the purpose of making a connection with the One who has all the answers to every prayer. Jesus/Yahshua is the way... The way to what? The way to the Father. He is seated at the right hand of the Father making intercession or petitioning on our behalf. As we recognize the Father, the Son and Holy Spirit in their rightful roles of the Godhead, we move closer to the perfect will of God. This is when we move into a whole new dimension of His presence. When this revelation becomes crystal clear to you, you will then understand what Jesus/Yahshua meant in John 17:21-23 (KJV) That they all may be one; as thou, Father, art in me, and I in thee, that they also may be one in us: that the world may believe that thou hast sent me. And the glory which thou gavest me I have given them; that they may be one, even as we are one: I in them, and thou in me, that they may be made perfect in one; and that the world may know that thou hast sent me, and hast loved them, as thou hast loved me.

In the dimension of God's perfect will, our bodies, which are subject to the laws of nature, all of a sudden come into the realm of the Spirit and are subject to the dynamics of the Almighty. Now, anything can happen! The blind see; the deaf hear; the lame walk, and the impossible becomes possible!

From the dimension of the perfect will of the Father, we can get a glimpse of the perspective of the Father. Let's view the cross from the Father's perspective. Most Christians see it as the place where God showed mercy on mankind. And while there is truth to that, we must understand that God has a plan; God has a *will*. The perspective of the Father allows us to see that worship was on His heart because the Father seeks such that will worship Him in Spirit and in truth. The Bible tells us that God turned His back on the Son because of the events that were transpiring at and by His own command. For that brief moment the world was thrust into utter darkness. For years, I have said that I believe God created the entire cosmos for the purpose of worship. Everything that God created,

47

everything that has transpired since the beginning of time is for the purpose of finding a people, a remnant that will worship Him in spirit and in truth. After all, it is evident that God wanted to be chosen because the Bible tells us that God walked with man in the Garden of Eden and fellowshipped with man. God was longing for fellowship, so He made man.

Luke 23:44-47 And it was about the sixth hour, and there was a darkness over all the earth until the ninth hour. And the sun was darkened, and the veil of the temple was rent in the midst. And when Jesus/Yahshua had cried with a loud voice, he said, Father, into thy hands I commend my spirit: and having said thus, he gave up the ghost. Now when the centurion saw what was done, he glorified God, saying, certainly this was a righteous man. The ultimate pain and suffering did not take place on the cross because by this time, Yahshua had already entered into the dimension where the Father's perfect will was done! His pain and suffering was in the Garden as he prayed for the Father's will to override his own. In obedience, he submitted to the Father's request and responded, "Nevertheless, not my will, but thy will be done." We know from Scripture that an angel came to strengthen him so that he could fulfill the Father's instruction. God's mercy was extended to His own son, and it reaches to everyone in all creation!

We experience life here on earth in the realm of four dimensions, but I believe there is a dimension where we enter into the protective, hovering glory of Holy Spirit, where Holy Spirit guards all that belongs to the Father like a mother hen brooding over her chicks. It sounds like Holy Spirit met Jesus/Yahshua in the Garden of Gethsemane and supernaturally strengthened him. In the book of Genesis, the Bible speaks of the earth being without form covered by darkness and Holy Spirit hovered over the waters. The word hovered means waiting for action. The moment you move towards the will of the Father, Holy Spirit will hover over you waiting for action on your part, and then Holy Spirit will carry you.

CHAPTER FIVE
THE FIFTH DIMENSION

When God brought the Israelites out of Egypt, their future had already been laid out by God's providential plan. The problem with the children of Israel was not where they came from or where they had been. The problem was in their minds! It was easier for God to deliver them out of Egypt than it was to deliver them from their own minds. Open up your mind, and receive the many revelations in this book. Uncharted and unknown as they may seem, they are biblically founded and biblically solid.

The Bible speaks of the fourth watch, and I don't think I've ever heard anyone teach on this topic. This was divine revelation to me. Matthew 14:25 (KJV) And in the fourth watch of the night Jesus/Yahshua went unto them, walking on the sea. The fourth watch is around 3:00 AM, and there is something to be discovered here. Christ tapped into a supernatural power available only in this time zone that eventually led to him walking on water!

Daniel 8:13-14 Then I heard a holy one speaking; and another holy one said to that certain one who was speaking, "How long will the vision be, concerning the daily sacrifices and the transgression of desolation, the giving of both the sanctuary and the host to be trampled underfoot?" And he said to me, "For two thousand three hundred days;[a] then the sanctuary shall be cleansed." A revelation of a prophetic event was shown to Daniel by a holy angel; and then, another angel asked a question concerning *numbers*? He asked, "How long?" The name of that angel is displayed in the Hebrew and is placed in the margin. His name is "PALMONI," and it means *the numberer of secrets*, or *the wonderful numberer*." Palmoni was assigned by the Almighty to be the keeper of numbers.

Everything God created has a calculable number and fits in with God's mathematics. The study of numerology dates back to ancient times, and each letter in the Hebrew language has a numeric value and meaning all its own. The study of numerology and Bible code, or the hidden meanings of words in Scripture, is called gematria.

According to gematria or Bible code, the pattern and shape of the number 4 represents a link between our dimension and God's dimension of His perfect will. It represents the bridge between the natural and the 5th dimension. The 5th dimension is a dimension of light that is inconceivable to the human mind.

When the pattern of the number four appears to us as a symbol, it represents God linking us into the dimension of His perfect will. It represents the bridge between the natural and the 5th dimension where we are surrounded by His presence and overtaken by His perfect will. This is the dimension Jesus/Yahshua tapped into and walked on water!

The fifth dimension is a dimension of light. This is the place where the glory of God resides! The word "glory" in the Hebrew is *kawbowd*, which means the full weight of something, honor, abundance, splendor, dignity, and reputation. Imagine walking in a realm where honor, abundance, splendor, dignity, and reputation are the standard. Anything could happen! As believers, we peek through the keyhole and think we have access and understanding, but in reality, God's glory is unfathomable in its splendor and opulence.

50

We tap into the light source of God's creative energy when we align ourselves with His perfect will. It is like unlocking a vault. When the light of God's glory pierces through the keyhole, it is like trillions of wattages of light beaming through. That is the glory! In the glory, what you need is done and already perfected. This realm is not always accessible. There are portals in time that are opened up to those who are aware, watchful, and awake. Jesus/Yahshua said, "I am the light of the world..." In essence, it's like he was saying I am the portal, I am the way... Remember when Jesus/Yahshua was in the Garden of Gethsemane, he rebuked his disciples and said, "Could you not tarry one hour?" He was opening up a supernatural portal at that very hour! Christ opened up the realm where we could have access to these time portals into the 5th dimension of God's glory. If Jesus/Yahshua could enter into this dimension and walk through solid walls, then, we as the body of Christ, whom he also called the light of the world, can do likewise. You are the light of the world!

John 1:1 The light shineth into the darkness and the darkness overcame it not. And we beheld His glory, the glory as of the only begotten of the Father. We are called to carry the light of the glory of God just like Jesus/Yahshua did when he walked on the earth. There is a connection between light and physics that confirms why we are called to be the light of the world.

Have you ever studied physics? Research on black holes has produced a theory. Black holes are actually massive stars exhausting nuclear fuel that causes them to implode, actually cutting them away from the rest of the universe. When God spoke His will in the beginning, He said, "Let there be light!" and the light shot out from within Him and exploded into the expanding universes. God, in His infinite wisdom, mixed just enough gravitational pull into our universe so that light keeps expanding, and it does not collapse upon itself like the black hole. A black hole is not the absence of light, but the implosion of light so intense that it restructures itself into a black hole.

If you do not align yourself with God's supernatural laws of gravity, you will implode like the stars. A thought worth pondering: stars that become black holes are stars that are so full of their own magnetic force they collapse within themselves. How often do you hear Christians talking about how the devil did this and the devil did

51

that, when the real problem lies in that they are so full of their own ego, they implode within themselves. They become so full of themselves that they self-destruct. And yet, the majority of Christians blame the devil while they invest their entire focus to living their best lives now and becoming superstars!

I have watched as people have sat in our church services whose countenance reflected a disappointment when I refused to give Satan any credit or glory. One service, I mentioned a pastor friend of mine who had quit focusing on and preaching about the devil and he noticed the devil was almost nonexistent! I mentioned I was in agreement with his statement because I too believe that Jesus defeated Satan once and for all. The morning after that service, I noticed someone posted a picture of a demonic, devilish figure on Facebook with a stern warning. *"Those of you who do not believe the devil is real, you'd better start believing in him because he's going to come after you."* It sounded more like an advertisement to believe and have faith in the Devil! I am no novice when it comes to dealing with demonic powers, but my focus, my passion; my pursuit is His presence, not some devil. For years other pastors would send people who were dealing with demonic activity to my church. They heard that I exorcised demons, but in reality what I was doing was setting people free by the power of wisdom and knowledge and the anointing of worship and prayer. The bible says the anointing breaks the yoke. One young man was in a psych ward and his family begged me to go pray for him. I sat in a visitation room with him and began to pray the perfect prayer and within seconds, he straightened up and went from a zombie-like state to being completely coherent. When our visitation was up, the orderly came to me and said, "You are not allowed to do exorcisms here." I did not respond and thanked him. I was asked to wait in the waiting room and within an hour, they released the young man to me!

It is easy to underestimate the power of light, until you are without it or thrust into darkness! Normally, we do not give light a second thought because we expect it to be there when we awaken or when we flip the light switch. The interesting thing about light is that it gives our otherwise black and white world color! Without light there is no dimension of color. In the dark, everything is black and white; there is no color. Life would be lackluster without colors.

Many believers go through life living in black and white without even knowing it, simply because they are not aligned to God's perfect will. Black and white TVs were fine until Technicolor was introduced, and now, we have high definition televisions with intense color packages. Kind of like Dorothy in The Wizard of Oz, it's not until she is in the Land of Oz that color enters the perspective.

I believe God is a master mathematician where everything in the universe is calculable and adds up! There is a mathematical equation for everything that happens on earth. Everything in your life adds up for good or bad. When things do not add up for good, it is because you are trying to do God's "heaven-ometry" with your little two-plus-two simplistic mindset. All creation, from the simplest to the most complex can always be reduced to numbers. Pythagoras, the father of mathematics, discovered a great truth when he said "Numbers are the language of the universe." He wrote that the purpose of numbers is for investigating the universe. I couldn't agree more! God speaks the language of numbers!

James 1:17 Every good gift and every perfect gift is from above, and cometh down from the Father of lights, with whom is no variableness, neither shadow of turning. In order to tap into the resources of God's Kingdom, you must align yourself with His Word and enter into the dimension of His perfect will. He is the Father of lights! That means the dismal darkness of your situation has to yield to the brightness of His glory.

Getting back to the theory of black holes, the existence of black holes does not mean the absence of light; it simply means the light has moved into a different dimension. That is proof that God is willing to take us into different dimensions of His Kingdom if we open our minds. What does this mean to you right now? It means that you do not have to remain in your present state. If you are under oppression and stressed out, you can move into a different dimension of the Spirit and escape the repercussions of your present state.

Remember, God's will is a place found in the place of His presence. God's will is power. God's will is His Word. God's will is His name! You can access every human need through the dimension of His perfect will! 2 Peter 1: 3 (KJV) According as his divine power hath given unto us all things that pertain unto life and godliness, through the knowledge of him that hath called us to glory and virtue...

The Perfect Prayer positions you mentally, spiritually, physically and emotionally for the manifestation of the impossible. We all miss the mark at times, and then wonder why things don't quite add up. It is no wonder when many believers do not tithe; they seldom give offerings and are clueless when it comes to sowing seeds. Most every believer I know is familiar with Galatians 6:7 (KJV) 7 Be not deceived; God is not mocked: for whatsoever a man soweth, that shall he also reap.

God established a reward system through the principles of tithes and offerings. Tithing is like your spiritual life insurance. It is part of what aligns you to God's perfect will. The curse of holding on to your tithes and offerings is not some evil action initiated by God; it is a natural law in the Kingdom. It goes into effect when you operate out of rebellion and greed. By the same token, a natural law opens when you obey and release your tithes and offerings.

Allow me to explain some differences regarding tithes, offerings, sowing seeds and offering up a sacrifice. According to Malachi chapter three, tithes and offerings are a command; seeds and sacrifices are optional. You decide if you want to offer up a seed and or sacrificial offering. The difference between a seed and a sacrifice is, a seed is a living gift and a sacrifice is burned at the altar. What does this mean for the sons of God?

Malachi 3: 6-14 (AMP) For I am the Lord, I do not change; that is why you, O sons of Jacob, are not consumed. Even from the days of your fathers you have turned aside from My ordinances and have not kept them. Return to me, and I will return to you, says the Lord of hosts. But you say, How shall we return? Will a man rob or defraud God? Yet you rob and defraud Me. But you say, In what way do we rob or defraud You? [You have withheld your] tithes and offerings. You are cursed with the curse, for you are robbing Me, even this whole nation. Bring all the tithes (the whole tenth of your income) into the storehouse, that there may be food in My house, and prove Me now by it, says the Lord of hosts, if I will not open the windows of heaven for you and pour you out a blessing, that there shall not be room enough to receive it. And I will rebuke the devourer [insects and plagues] for your sakes and he shall not destroy the fruits of your ground, neither shall your vine drop its fruit before the time in the field, says the Lord of hosts. And all nations shall call you happy and blessed, for you shall be a land of delight, says the Lord of hosts. Your words have been strong and hard against Me, says the Lord. Yet you say, What have we spoken against You? You have said, It is useless to serve God, and what profit is it if we keep His ordinances and walk gloomily and as if in mourning apparel before the Lord of hosts?

Undoubtedly, you have probably heard teachings on the topic of tithes and offerings from your pastor, your local Christian television host or maybe you made the discovery on your own as you studied the Scriptures. Every teaching I have heard on the topic has always focused on the part about God opening up the windows of heaven and pouring out a blessing that one cannot contain. However, the understanding that God will rebuke the devourer on our behalf is an even more powerful visual of God's protection through the power of the tithe. Tithing is like paying your homeowner's insurance. You don't necessarily receive a benefit from your insurance until catastrophe strikes, and then, the peace of mind knowing you are covered is priceless! You've no doubt seen many of the insurance companies' commercials: "You're in good hands with Allstate." "Like a good neighbor State Farm is there." You don't really have need for catastrophic insurance until you are hit with the perfect storm, and everything you own goes up in smoke, is pummeled by hail or decimated by a tornado.

The tithe opens the windows of heaven, and the offerings release the pouring out of the blessing you cannot contain. What good is opening up a window if there is no cool air flowing? The same principle is evident here. Your tithe opens the window, and then, your offerings, or firstfruits activate the blessing of the cool breeze. Finally, your seed rebukes the devourer! Can you see the progression that so many miss? It's not enough to simply give a little here and a little there; you must adhere to the instructions established by God for generations. This is the only place where God encourages us to prove him. Malachi 3:10 (KJV) Prove me now herewith, see if I will not open up the windows of heaven...

Have you ever seen a shaft of light shooting out from the heavens on a cloudy day? Imagine the light of God's glory doing the same when you honor the LORD with your tithes and offerings. You could be in a sealed up tomb under the depths of the sea, and God could send a portal to shine down on your situation. When His light shines, everything changes. When you have experienced the light of His presence, your countenance changes. Under His supernatural light, you will change! All you have to do is come out of your superstar mentality and come under His authority. What does this have to do with numbers and Palmoni? It's all about the 10%, the amount of the first-fruit, the amount of the seed you sow. It's about the numbers!

Mark 4: 20 (ESV) But those that were sown on the good soil are the ones who hear the word and accept it and bear fruit, thirtyfold and sixtyfold and a hundredfold. Some will reap 30, 60, 100 fold return! Numbers, numbers, numbers! The fourth book of the Bible is called Numbers!

I do not know too many people who are overly, abundantly blessed. Even the abundantly wealthy Oprah Winfreys and Martha Stewarts of this world are not too blessed that they are satisfied. They continue working, creating and striving for more. I watched an interview with the Harry Potter mogul-author where she was asked if she felt abundantly blessed and secure that she would never lack for anything for the rest of her life. Her response was shocking, albeit honest. She said she did not feel secure because she was afraid she could lose it all. The greatest danger of contentment is losing creativity to produce and desire more. Prayer is really more for the one praying than the One we pray to.

We are physiologically designed according to God's plan and His divine order. Each human life is designed in accordance with the divine code or the golden mean. Mathematically, our bodies are aligned with the equation and the rhythms of the supernatural realm. This prayer does nothing to move God; instead, it aligns us mentally to comprehend that He is in heaven and not here in this realm, in the midst of our mess. Where is the Kingdom? Jesus/Yahshua said, "The Kingdom of God is within you." That implies that it is in the realm of the supernatural and not in the natural. We begin the prayer (Our heavenly Father...) by establishing that He is in heaven, recognizing that we are on Earth. Now, we have connected earth to heaven! Scientifically, we now know that there are many universes. We should feel honored that out of all the universes God chose Earth for mankind to inhabit. The psalmist penned it quite eloquently, "What is man that thou are mindful of him?" The Spirit of God opens up the heavens to bless you just like God's Word says in Malachi 3:10b ...prove me now herewith, saith the LORD of hosts, if I will not open you the windows of heaven, and pour you out a blessing, that there shall not be room enough to receive it.

There is something supernaturally powerful about the Aramaic translation of the LORD'S Prayer. It transforms us and transports us into a new dimension in the Spirit realm. Zechariah 4:6b (KJV) Not by might, nor by power, but by my spirit, saith the Lord of hosts. The greatest works the church will ever see and know are in the dimension of the supernatural.

Have you ever tried to make something happen by your own power and means? We must learn not to be moved by what we see, hear, smell, taste, or touch. We must begin to look at things from the dimension of the Spirit, power and authority. Our five senses are for navigating on this earth. It is only when we align our whole being with God's will that we unlock the full power and authority God promised. John 1:12 (KJV) says, to them gave he the power to become the sons of God... 1 John 5:4 (NASB) For whatever is born of God overcomes the world...

Every situation you are faced with must become subject to the Word of God. When sickness, disease or lack attempt to come against you, you can stand against it with the power of the Word of God resident within you. When you position yourself in the realm of the Spirit and pray, it is like moving into the dimension of angels. In space, things work differently. In space, men can float; men can fly! I love watching the astronauts who live in the space station as they float around in their spacecraft. Imagine for a moment what they must feel as they float around: weightless, unencumbered, feeling limitless, feeling ultimate freedom. As in heaven, so also on earth...

No one is completely certain how many dimensions there are, but we know Who created all dimensions. If we know who created them, then, we have a sure shot at gaining access to these dimensions as we obediently navigate through different levels. The Bible tells us we go from glory to glory, precept upon precept and line upon line. Religion endeavors to place God in a box, but of course, we know that is impossible! God is so great; He is not containable by anything we can imagine or invent. Scripture refers to His eyes, His hands, His voice as if He were human, but it is simply for aiding our feeble minds in imagining His greatness. The Bible also says His greatness is unsearchable. God is not a man; He is neither male nor female, but we reference Him as male because it helps us understand His role as our Father.

Ephesians 3:20 (KJV) Now unto him that is able to do exceeding abundantly above all that we ask or think, according to the power that worketh in us... God is more than what we can ask or think or even imagine. His greatness exceeds our understanding and He goes beyond the dimensions known to us. The book of Romans gives us a glimpse into, what I believe are, some of the dimensions that we can experience. The Apostle Paul, who experienced time travel, was caught up in the dimension of the supernatural, confidently lists 10 different experiences as he writes in Romans 8:38-39 (AMP) For I am convinced [and continue to be convinced—beyond any doubt] that neither <u>death,</u> nor <u>life,</u> nor <u>angels,</u> nor <u>principalities,</u> nor <u>things present</u> *and* <u>threatening,</u> nor <u>things to come,</u> nor <u>powers,</u> nor <u>height,</u> nor <u>depth,</u> nor <u>any other created thing,</u> will be able to separate us from the [unlimited] love of God, which is in Christ Jesus/Yahshua our Lord.

It was only 10 verses prior that he wrote, "All things work together for good..." He apparently had access to different dimensions to make a statement like that.

Scientists have discovered that they have the ability to detect or comprehend at least 10 different dimensions. In this passage, there are 10 different dimensions that cannot separate us from the dimension where God lives. The place where God lives has to be absolute sheer love. No dimension can keep us from the place of His sheer love: the place of His presence.

When we enter into a dimension beyond the four dimensions of our world: height, length, depth and time, we move into a dimension unaffected by the present. The Perfect Prayer takes you into a dimension of the supernatural where everything changes. You could drive the same route you have driven to work for years, and everything appear differently. When you move into the fifth dimension, even by the sheer nature of the number five which represents grace and favor, you move into a dimension of believing you are blessed! You think differently; you perceive things differently, and you respond to things in a different way. It is not mind over matter or living like the proverbial ostrich with its head stuck in the sand. It is seeing things through the eyes of faith:

through God's eyes. The understanding of moving into the fifth dimension gives you a different perspective on otherwise negative, hopeless situations.

I remember hearing a song growing up, which the church I attended considered taboo because the lyrics implied a connection to the astrological world. I have never been into horoscopes, but I believe there is something that changes when things align themselves with the patterns and rhythms of Holy Spirit. "All things work together..." to me, means that everything will align itself to change my circumstance. The song referenced the alignment of Jupiter and Mars and the age of Aquarius. Now, I don't know about Aquarius, but I know that the ONE who hung the sun, moon, planets, and stars in the universe can change everything by the power of His Word. We know enough about cosmology to understand that light travels at 186,000 miles per second. It travels that fast because it follows the path of least resistance.

God opens up His shafts of light that I like to call portals of glory. God uses light because it is the most agreeable of all His creations. In the beginning, God spoke and He said, "Let there be light!" and the light obeyed and exploded into all the universes. When He spoke those words, the light never stopped expanding itself. God spoke to me and said, "I'm going to send the light of my Word, the light of my glory to heal your diseases. I'm going to turn your life around; I'm going to place you in another dimension of power and authority, honor and character, but you must be as submissive and agreeable as the light." When the Spirit of the LORD says, "Move," we must be ready to move. If light travels at 186,000 miles per second, think how fast God moves. It gives new meaning to the Scripture, "...I will *hasten* my Word to perform it." (Jeremiah 1:12 KJV)

Daniel 10: 5-12 (AMP) I lifted up my eyes and looked, and behold, a man clothed in linen, whose loins were girded with pure gold of Uphaz. His body also was [a golden luster] like beryl, his face had the appearance of lightning, his eyes were like flaming torches, his arms and his feet like glowing burnished bronze, and the sound of his words was like the noise of a multitude [of people or the roaring of the sea]. And I, Daniel, alone saw the vision [of this heavenly being], for the men who were with me did not see the vision, but a great trembling fell upon them so that they fled to hide

59

themselves. So I was left alone and saw this great vision, and no strength was left in me, for my fresh appearance was turned to pallor; I grew weak *and* faint [with fright]. Then I heard the sound of his words; and when I heard the sound of his words, I fell on my face in a deep sleep, with my face [sunk] to the ground. And behold, a hand touched me, which set me [unsteadily] upon my knees and upon the palms of my hands. And [the angel] said to me, O Daniel, you greatly beloved man, understand the words that I speak to you and stand upright, for to you I am now sent. And while he was saying this word to me, I stood up trembling. Then he said to me, Fear not, Daniel, for from the first day that you set your mind *and* heart to understand and to humble yourself before your God, your words were heard, and I have come as a consequence of [and in response to] your words.

When we align ourselves and our words with the dimensions of God's glory, we will have an uninterrupted, direct connection to His presence. In His presence, not even the Prince of Persia can stop the answer to Daniel's prayer. **The efficacy of The Perfect Prayer is supported by the power of the Word of God. It is backed by the millennia of ancient wisdom that has come before us.** God always confirms His Word.

Notice this powerful prayer ends with a connection that goes beyond forever and forever, as is traditionally recorded. To say, "to the end of the universe of all the universes" implies there are multiple time zones. Scientifically, we understand things that have happened to us have not yet happened out there because of the distance. That is why we are instructed to believe the report of the LORD. Where He dwells, we are not sick; we have no lack; we have no worries.

Only with the light of God's glory can we expect the answer to travel at or above 186,000 miles per second the – speed of light. I am sure there is not one reader reading this book that would not agree they want God to answer their prayers at the speed of light.

There are dimensions to His power that have not yet been unlocked because we do not know enough about them yet. Many believers find themselves on the short end of the stick when it comes to the dimensions of God's Spirit. When you have not seen these dimensions at work in yours or someone else's life, it is a struggle entering in.

Dimensions imply parameters, boundaries and limitations, while dominion has neither boundaries nor limitations. When you look at a picture, you see what is within the parameters: the height, width and depth of the size of the frame. These three dimensions signify parameters, and parameters signify boundaries. Boundaries restrict and prohibit entry, and where there is limitation dominion has no value. Merriam Webster's Dictionary defines the word "dominion" as having supreme authority, and absolute ownership. Imagine the endless possibilities when the boundaries to your dimensions align with the supreme authority given to all within the Kingdom. Within the time zone of timelessness and boundlessness of Holy Spirit, God does things only He can do. It is at these moments when what you speak coincides with what God, and only God, can do. This is why Scripture says you can call those things, which be not, as though they were even as the prophets of old did. This dominion/supreme authority is exclusively performed within the glory of God.

We live within the perimeters or dimensions of earth, also known as the third dimension. Allow me to explain briefly. In our earthly atmosphere, there are three dimensions: height, depth and breadth. The power of The Perfect Prayer is what this chapter is all about. The prayer is like a secret code or password that provides passage into the other dimensions, ultimately culminating with divine dominion. The Perfect Prayer leads you through three different dimensions as you close out the prayer. *"For yours is the Kingdom, the power, and the glory..."* The first level is the *Kingdom*, which Christ said is within us, here on earth. *Power* is the next dimension or level; this is the realm of the heavenlies where the principalities and powers exist. And then we close out with *"glory"* that leads you straight into His presence!

Many believe because they are in the presence of the LORD or the presence of Holy Spirit that they have attained the apex or final dimension of God. You can be in the presence of someone great; however, you may be among tens of thousands of people and not have the ability to communicate or touch the celebrated one personally. It is not until you are granted audience that you have access with not only His presence and His person, but with His glory! The dimension of His person is the fourth dimension. When you move past the first, second and third dimensions and enter into the fourth dimension of His person, you are now before Him. He is reachable, touchable and attainable. This is the place of dominion. You can decree anything, and it shall be.

WISDOM PRINCIPLE: THE PLACE OF DOMINION IS IN HIS PERFECT WILL.

In the beginning of the prayer, there is an acknowledgment of His holiness, His name, His Kingdom and finally His will. His will is the fourth dimension of His person and of dominion. The laws that are familiar to us do not govern the fourth dimension because His will is sovereign. The boundaries of other dimensions are subject to His will. Nothing hinders the will of the Father. His will *is* done. His will subjugates all other dimensions. When wisdom and understanding come together in agreement and align themselves in our lives, we give birth to God's perfect, predestined will for our lives.

The prayer closes out with a different concept of time from the popularized version, which says, *"For thine is the kingdom, the power and the glory, forever and ever. Amen."* The Aramaic states, *"For Yours is the Kingdom, the power and the glory, to the end of the universe all of universes. Amen."* It is a known fact that when God spoke the universes into existence, they never stopped expanding. Forever and ever is tied to a timeline, timeframe or a time zone, as opposed to the universe of all universes, which never stop expanding and never will. This goes beyond the scope of time. We have to move from the dimension of the earthly kingdom to the realm of power (principalities), and then, move up one more level into the dimension of His glory, which places us in the fourth dimension. Now, we are moving past the glory into another dimension altogether. There is a realm, a place, beyond His glory!

The significance of the number four will help you understand the possibilities that are inherent within the fourth dimension. The number four, according to numerology, stands for creation. It is the number of material completeness. On the fourth day of creation, all that is material was created. The earth is governed by four great elements: earth, wind/air, fire and water. There are four regions of the earth: north, south, east and west. Your day has four parts: morning, noon, evening and midnight. There are four seasons in a year: winter, spring, summer and fall. There are four variations of the lunar phases. The number four is the first number, which is not a prime and the first divisible number. It stands for dividing as in the parting of the Red Sea. Even our own independence as Americans was settled on the fourth day of the seventh month.

Psalm 91:1 (KJV) He that dwelleth in the secret place of the most High shall abide under the shadow of the Almighty. Psalm 91 gives us an understanding of dimensions. Paul was transported into a supernatural, secret location by way of the secret place of the Most High. In this place, physical things can move at the speed of light. When we move into this dimension, it is possible to experience supernatural transportation. In other words, the physics that would normally apply to our natural world become suspended and overpowered, so that the dimension of the supernatural takes precedence.

A perfect portrait of this supernatural dimension appears in John 7 as Jesus/Yahshua and his disciples prepare to observe the Feast of Tabernacles. He fully intends to participate in the Holy Days; however, he has to go in incognito. There is a shroud of mystery that follows Christ wherever he goes.

Psalm 91:1 (KJV) He that dwelleth in the secret place of the Most High shall abide under the shadow of the Almighty... Christ moved into the dimension that made him invisible to those who were looking for him. He aligned himself with the power and energy of the Father and moved into the fifth dimension, the dimension of light that travels at the speed of 186,000 miles per second.

John 7:8 (AMP) Go up to the feast yourselves. I am not going up to this feast because My time has not yet fully come. Remember, this was in the middle of the Feast of Tabernacles or the Feast of Booths. Jesus/Yahshua was making a transition from the fourth dimension into the fifth dimension. In verse twenty-nine, John refers to Christ as not having come into his hour. Hour deals with an appointed time, and time denotes spontaneity. Jesus/Yahshua refers to this timeless zone in the book of John chapter seven by saying, "Yet a little while I am with you and then I go to Him who sent me. You will look for me, but you won't find me because where I am going you cannot go." The Pharisees were baffled, "Where is he going that we cannot go? Is he just going to disappear?" At the end of the Feast of Tabernacles, at the most climactic moment in verse 37 he screams out, "Is anybody thirsty? If you believe in me, drink of the rivers of living waters that flow out of your bellies."

Holy Spirit had not yet been sent and Jesus/Yahshua, the Son of Man, was still a mere man; his heavenly Father had not yet glorified him. He had not yet reached "the full weight of who he was." His body had not yet been glorified. Why would he have needed to go into these dimensions if he was already in a god-like state?

Why would he need to go in secret to the Feast of Tabernacles? Could it be that he became fearless and bold on the last day of the feast because he had entered into the fifth dimension? In verse 40, when the people saw something they had not seen before, they said, "Surely, this man is a prophet." They thought he was Elijah reincarnated. Then, there were those who recognized him as the Christ, the Messiah. They questioned, "Wait a minute, if he is the Messiah, what is he doing coming from Galilee? Doesn't Scripture state that the Messiah will come from the lineage of David, and he's from Bethlehem? In the fourth chapter of Luke, Yahshua is driven from the temple and almost thrown off a cliff. The Bible says he walked right *through* the crowd. Here, Yahshua enters the dimension of the Spirit with the power of the Holy Ghost. He escaped death because he moved into the realm of God's glory, which is located in the fifth dimension.

Jesus/Yahshua healed people, not on the basis of their sickness or their need, but rather because of his compassion. Not to mention, sickness and disease do not exist in the perfect will of God. He dealt with the genetic codes and with the flawed genetic transference of humanity based on human error and wrong choices. He healed and cast out devils based on generational curses. He dealt with the root of each problem.

In part, understanding the timing of prayer requires that we recognize there are seasons for making petition for certain things. Naturally, if there is sickness and disease, we can bring those needs to the Father at any time. Again, it is not about asking for a miracle or a harvest from a seed we have sown; it has to do with the alignment of the genetics of each individual with the perfect will of

God. Each chromosome lines up with the divine will of the Great Architect and Designer of all that is.

With prayer, there are seasons for harvesting just like the four seasons: winter, spring, summer and fall. You cannot harvest in the winter; you must be in sync with the order of the seasons. This is why some people become disillusioned. They are sowing in a season of harvesting because their time of sowing is off, but eventually, harvest season will roll around again, and you will reap if you faint not! As with Jesus/Yahshua, when he told his mother, "It is not yet my time…" he was waiting for his season of miracles to begin.

Many passages in Scripture contain the words, "The hour is coming…" It is obvious that this has to do with *timing*. I learned an interesting thing about bells and clocks the other day. Originally, bells were created and designed to announce the call to prayer. When the bells rang, the early Americans knew it was time to pray. Later, timepieces were designed, not to keep time or tell us what time it is; again, they were designed to signal the hour of prayer.

There is no doubt that prayer is something inspired by God and not man. The LORD'S Prayer, which is so universally recited and often sentimentally entrenched with human affection, is the model prayer and outline for effective prayer. It is simply a matter of knowing the timing of prayer. Christ could have taught this prayer at the beginning of his journey with his disciples, but he waited for the right moment to reveal the secret to prayer.

Matthew 6:6-8 (KJV) But thou, when thou prayest, enter into thy closet, and when thou hast shut thy door, pray to thy Father which is in secret; and thy Father which seeth in secret shall reward thee openly. But when ye pray, use not vain repetitions, as the heathen do: for they think that they shall be heard for their much speaking. Be not ye therefore like unto them: for your Father knoweth what things ye have need of, before ye ask him.

The Father already knows what you need before you even ask. Prayer is for the purpose of convincing YOURSELF that His will is already done! Jesus/Yahshua knows all about effective prayer. Every prayer he offered to the Father was answered except for one. You're probably thinking every prayer he ever uttered was answered. The only time the Father did not answer his prayer was when he asked for something that was not in accordance with God's will. In Matthew 26:39, he prayed, "Father, let this cup pass from

65

me…" He did not receive an answer because he did not pray the Father's will; he prayed his own, and not until he shifted from his will and said, "Nevertheless, not my will, but your will *is* done!" Too often, we become disillusioned because God does not answer a prayer, and yet, the Messiah experienced the very same emotions and even frustrations.

When Christ enters the Feast of Tabernacles, something changes. Where he had previously wanted to remain incognito, now, he had stepped into the midst of the crowd with a totally different attitude. His time had finally come! His time was at hand! He shouts boldly over the crowd, "Is anyone thirsty?" Notice the shift in his position as a public figure. Prior to this incident, he wanted to remain anonymous and did not want to be discovered. Perhaps, because there were those who wanted to bring him harm. Now, he is not only speaking as the son of Mary and Joseph, but he speaks as a prophet.

This chapter may sound to you like smoke and mirrors, and sadly, there are many believers who would readily believe in magic tricks than believe that there is a secret dimension of the Spirit available to us. In John 8:59 the Bible says that Jesus/Yahshua's accusers tried to stone him, but he walked right through the crowd, and they did not see him. Jesus/Yahshua had aligned himself with the energy and the power of the Father and moved into a dimension where he became invisible to those who were seeking to do him harm. Another example of this is found in Luke 4:29-30 (NIV) They got up, drove him out of the town, and took him to the brow of the hill on which the town was built, in order to throw him off the cliff. But he walked right through the crowd and went on his way.

The Messiah theology is the very fiber of Judaism. As Jesus/Yahshua became more and more familiar to the crowds, men began to debate whether He was the long awaited Messiah. People began to question his origins because the Torah is very clear about the coming Messiah being from a certain city and of a certain lineage. The crowd became hostile, and they sought to kill him by throwing him over a cliff, nevertheless, Christ walked right in their midst and became invisible! As he moved into this fifth dimension, he was able to make a miraculous escape from the angry crowd. The Father made provision for Jesus/Yahshua in this dimension and just as he made provision for His Son, He will make provision for you!

This is the dimension where things move at the speed of

light. This is the dimension where your faith is launched into a whole new level, and your eyes see what others cannot. If something were to move past you at the speed of light, would you be able to see it? Of course not! The fifth dimension, the secret place of The Most High, has always been available to us. We just have not had eyes or understanding to see. It is only our belief systems that impede us from gaining access to the same experiences as Christ.

Ephesians 1:17 (NIV) I keep asking that the God of our Lord Jesus/Yahshua Christ, the glorious Father, may give you the Spirit of wisdom and revelation, so that you may know him better. I pray that *the eyes of your heart may be enlightened...* Everything that you need lies hidden in this dimension. It is within reach; you just cannot see it, yet! God moves and operates at the speed of light because He is light! I believe there is more happening in the realm of the unseen than the realm of the seen. Because in the fifth dimension, which is as close as the air you are breathing at this very moment, every need, want and wish is within reach. You don't have to wait to tap into this dimension until you are in dire straights. Simply, align yourself with the realm and dimension of Holy Spirit.

It was Holy Spirit who led Christ throughout his life and even led him into the desert. Holy Spirit led Jesus/Yahshua into the wilderness so that His faith could be proven. It was Holy Spirit who hovered over Mary when she conceived the Messiah in her mortal womb. It was Holy Spirit who hovered over Jesus/Yahshua's body while he lay dead in the tomb. Holy Spirit is your connection to the fifth dimension. Peter did more in one day after he received Holy Spirit in the Upper Room than he did walking side by side with Jesus/Yahshua for three years. To come into God's presence is more than just feeling goose bumps; it is coming into His perfect will and receiving instruction to navigate through the realm of the unseen—the fifth dimension.

CHAPTER SIX
TO WHOM ARE YOU PRAYING?

...your Father knoweth what things ye have need of, before ye ask him. Matthew 6:32 KJV The question remains, to whom are you making your needs known? Most people I know talk to Jesus/Yahshua and ask him to go here and there, even though the Bible clearly tells us he is *seated* at the right hand of the Father making intercession for us all. Jesus/Yahshua said, "When ye pray, pray in this manner. Our Heavenly Father..." He did not say our heavenly Jesus/Yahshua... Perhaps, this sounds like a matter of semantics, but did you really grasp what I said at the close of the previous chapter? The only prayer that Jesus/Yahshua ever prayed that did not get answered was when he prayed his own will, when he was in the Garden of Gethsemane! Perhaps, you are thinking that the Father is the same as the Son and the Son is the same as Holy Spirit and Holy Spirit is the same as the Father, etc. However, it is quite clear that each person of the Godhead has a role and an individual personality.

I wonder how many believers actually realize that Christianity and the Messiah came from Judaism. The Old

Testament is filled with instructions, directions and rituals that the Father established long before Christianity came into existence. In fact, the Bible refers to them as statutes and laws. Jesus/Yahshua followed all the Jewish laws and kept all the Jewish feasts. He said, "If you love me *keep my commandments...*" Christ had two commandments, and they were both related to love. Mark 12:29 (AMP) Jesus/Yahshua answered, "The first and most important one is: 'Hear, O Israel, the Lord our God is one LORD; and you shall love the LORD your God with all your heart, and with all your soul (life), and with all your mind (thought, understanding), and with all your strength.' This is the second: 'You shall [unselfishly] love your neighbor as yourself.' There is no other commandment greater than these." Christ was very clear about keeping these two commandments, for in keeping these two, we keep all of them.

God is doing a sovereign work in Christendom. It is not something people have prayed for, asked for or believed for. It is a sovereign work from the Father's heart! He is strengthening and making visible the tie between Judaism and Christianity. I am Jewish on both my mother and father's families and have been studying and keeping most of the Jewish feasts for much of my life. Presently, we are approaching Yom Kippur, also known as the Day of Atonement – the holiest day of the year. In Old Testament days, the priest was allowed to enter into the Holy of Holies once a year, and he was granted the right to speak the most holy, ineffable name of YAHVEH to make atonement for the Israelites. He did not go into the Holy chamber to pray; he entered the chamber prepared with incense ready to carry out the protocol of worship established by the Almighty.

There are two testaments or covenants – the Old and New Testaments; new does not mean that the old is irrelevant; yet, this mindset comprises the ideals of many Christians today. I have experienced many different movements in the Kingdom over the past few decades. In that time, I have never heard anyone expound on the topic of God the Father, perhaps, because the focus has always been on Christ, His Son. I am not trying to diminish the role of Christ; however, it is greatly important to know whom you are praying to.

You've already heard me say over and over The Perfect

Prayer is all about alignment with *God's* perfect will. And yet, so many suffer and trudge through each day with ailments, pains and diseases we simply accept as normal. Sometimes, we get inspired and motivated; we stand in faith for healing, and after the moment has passed, we lend acceptance to our maladies and accept it as part of life. Each time we accept anything but divine health and prosperity, it diminishes the power of the One who has positioned Himself as our Father, our Covering, our Shelter, our High Tower, our Deliverer, and our Healer. It is God's will for you to be healed! It is God's will for you to be whole! It is God's will for you to prosper and reap in accordance to what you sow!

An entirely different dimension of the Kingdom of God is opened to us when we experience the perfect will of God. To be in His perfect will means to stand in His presence, His flow, His timing, His schedule, His perfectly timed seasons. So then, why are there still so many sick and impoverished Christians among us? In the dimension of His perfect will, your sickness, your lack and your circumstances cannot and do not exist!

The word protocol means: the behavioral processes of – in this case a simple, yet profound prayer. Your behavior determines your access to His perfect will, to His favor, to divine health. Behavior means actions, deeds, demeanor or how you carry yourself. Your disposition can affect your prayer life!

Christ is who he is because of his willing obedience and self-denial, even unto death! He never drew attention to himself; instead, he directed all glory to his Father. Jesus/Yahshua is never quoted saying, "Worship me." His behavior gave him access to the Father who ultimately crowned him King of kings and gave him a seat at His right hand.

Christ had to follow the protocol to approach the Father; he in turn taught the disciples through a simple prayer that even a five year old could understand. One of my nieces, Kristen Ariel, was faced with a situation while in school. She had to take a state reading test to evaluate her reading skills. This presented a monumental challenge to her six-year-old mind. She was not doing well in reading because grandparents, who did not place much importance on academia, were raising her. She was basically illiterate. Alone at school, without assistance from family or friends, she had but one choice. She had memorized the perfect prayer. Pushing past her apprehension, with the faith of a six year old, she began to recite The LORD'S Prayer under her breath, trusting that God would rescue her if she simply placed herself in the middle of His perfect will. Kristen experienced something that cannot be accessed through academia or intellect. She recited the prayer and stepped into a dimension where illiteracy does not exist – a dimension where she had perfect comprehension. She was able to read her book aloud and passed with flying colors!

If we could only trust with the innocence of a child as we present ourselves before God, we could align ourselves with His dimension where His will is done on earth! Earth will line up with what is already made perfect and complete in the supernatural. Perhaps, this is why Jesus/Yahshua said, "Come as a little child." We are not required to understand God's logic. It just is. A six year old tapped into the currents of favor in heaven by simply knowing to *whom* she was praying. From that defining moment in my sweet niece's life, she has developed into a straight 'A' student. She is now in high school and continues to do well with her studies and is very talented.

In God's dimension, where His absolute perfect will is complete, time does not exist. In this dimension, you are complete, whole, finished! You are not a work in progress. The One to whom you pray makes all the difference. All of Earth aligns itself with heaven when you pray to the Father, the Creator of all that is.

Ask yourself why you have not reached the place in God where the situations that need perfecting in your personal life are not yet complete. Ask yourself, "Why have I not reached the place where I no longer worry about the circumstances that surround me, where the opinions of others no longer affect my day?" Why have I not arrived at the place where people are healed in my shadow, where signs, wonders and miracles follow me? Could it be that you have not arrived at the place because it is still all about you instead of the Father's will?

These are tough questions that I have asked myself despite living my entire life pursuing the things of God. I have come to the conclusion and agree with what the Bible says, "it's the traditions of men that make the word of God ineffective." Even the Apostle Paul conceded to his own questions regarding his own inadequacy. This is the man whom God dramatically snatched from a deep-rooted traditional belief system. Paul admitted his earthly struggles and admonished himself regarding the thorn in his side. And it was his understanding of the Father and not reasoning that got him to the place where he could say, "His grace is sufficient."

I believe the perfect will of God goes beyond our traditions and legalisms of religion. Every time we parade ourselves before the presence of the Almighty, asking Him to do our bidding, we are denying His sovereignty. We want what we want, when we want it and when our words fall powerless before God, we question, "Why God, why?" What we pray must be in alignment with His will.

In the meantime, we direct our worship upward and don't know if we are worshiping, God, Jesus, Holy Spirit or all three. Are we missing something here? I have a handsome, talented son, whom I am always proud of and am well pleased with him, despite the fact that he usually calls on his mother before me. What if all the members of the church I pastor directed all their needs and questions to my young son? Instinctively, he would point them back to his father, who is the pastor of the church, the man in charge, and this is what we see Christ doing during his tenure on the earth. Time and again, Jesus/Yahshua directed all attention to his Father.

John 11:41b (NIV) …Then Jesus/Yahshua looked up and said, "Father, I thank you that you have heard me. The implications in this passage lead me to believe that Jesus/Yahshua had already prayed and received an answer. He looked to the Father and prayed to the Father according to the Father's will and not His own and then simply gave thanks! Who are you praying to? If Christ is the great intercessor, the firstfruit of many, our example, and our Lord/Captain, as he is–so are we, don't you think we should follow in his footsteps?

Be honest; have you ever prayed for something specific and waited for the answer and never got what you wanted? Examine your petition. What is right and what is wrong with your prayer? Whose will did you ask for, your will or the Father's will? There is no higher authority than the will of the Father. When your petition is directed toward Christ, you have effectively stated that the sovereignty of the Father is of none effect. That may sound extreme, but 'the proof is in the pudding.'

The Bible says we should make our requests known in Jesus'/Yahshua's name. However, it is the Father who creates what we ask for. You place limitations to the answer, often allowing your petition to fall into stagnant territory when you pray amiss. Jesus/Yahshua can only acknowledge the Father and the Father's will. Yahshua is not going to do something outside the Father's will. The Father remains unmoved by your will or the will of anyone else, despite how great the need may be. The Father's Word is forever settled in heaven. In other words, it is the standard. When we move into the Father's will, even as Christ did, we move into a place of authority where even death is subject to our commands. No longer is your will done, but His will *is* done, "…as in heaven, so also on earth."

As Christians, we have probably all tossed around the word sovereignty or lauded God as sovereign. The word sovereign in Scripture means to have supreme authority, control and power over all that has happened, is happening and will happen. It means God has the right, the authority and the power to govern all that happens. What has occurred in the past, what is occurring now or what will occur in accordance to His divine will.

1 Chronicles 29:11-12 (ESV) Yours, O LORD, is the greatness and the power and the glory and the victory and the *majesty*, for all that is in the heavens and in the earth is yours. Yours is the *kingdom*, O Lord, and you are exalted as head above all. Both riches and honor come from you, and you rule over all. In your hand are *power* and *might*, and in your hand it is to make great and to give strength to all. Psalm 115:3 (ESV) Our God is in the heavens; he does all that he pleases. Proverbs 16:9 (ESV) The heart of man plans his way, but the Lord establishes his steps. Job 42:2 (ESV) I know that you can do all things, and that no purpose of yours can be thwarted. Isaiah 46:9-10 (ESV) Remember the former things of old; for I am God, and there is no other; I am God, and there is none like me, declaring the end from the beginning and from ancient times things not yet done, saying, 'My counsel shall stand, and I will accomplish all my purpose…' What marvelous imagery the Father provides for us to understand His sovereignty. His will accomplishes all His purposes.

The entire cosmos and all that exists were established through God's sovereignty. What He says *is*. It is a simple concept; there is no higher authority than His Word. He does not abdicate His throne for anyone or under any circumstance. He is sovereign! When

73

we come into agreement with the Word of the Father, we not only accept His sovereignty, but we establish His sovereignty in our lives. I am convinced that we have not seen the "mighty exploits" because we have not established God's authority as we ought. The Perfect Prayer establishes God's authority by instituting a foundation of God's sovereignty!

Daniel 11:32b (KJV) "…but the people that do know their God shall be strong, and do exploits…" Doesn't the Father already know what we need before we even ask? 2 Chronicles 16: 9 For the eyes of the Lord run to and fro throughout the whole earth, to show Himself strong on behalf of those whose heart is perfect toward Him. God is prepared and ready to show Himself strong on your behalf! He is sovereign, omnipresent, omniscient and omnipotent. He wants to reign sovereignly in your life, your home, your family, your job and in all your relationships. Talk to God; He's your Father and longs to hear from you. Direct your prayer to the Father, and He will move sovereignly and mightily in your life. It matters to whom you pray.

In the temple, only one priest could enter into the Holy of Holies during the High Holy Days. It was required that a rope be attached to his ankles so that he could be dragged out in the event of an emergency. I have heard preachers and teachers speculate it was because of the requirements to be spotless and holy before entering into the Holy of Holies. If the priest had any sin, he would surely die in the manifest presence of the LORD. However, I believe the priest would enter into the glory of the LORD and never want to leave! To enter into the holy chambers of the Most High is the ultimate point of worship – nothing else exists; why would you ever want to leave? Are you beginning to see the value in directing your prayer to the Father?

This past Sunday, we had a powerfully anointed time of worship, and I noticed that some of the parishioners were not participating. I heard Holy Spirit speak expressly to me. "If you don't open your mouth you cannot change anything. If you go to a restaurant and expect to eat something you like, something palatable to your taste, but never place your order, you cannot complain when you get nothing and still remain hungry." There are many in the kingdom of God who are hungry, but they refuse to open their mouths in worship and praise. You must open your mouth and speak

74

what you want.

When you begin to understand and fully grasp the importance of addressing the right person of the Godhead, you will become untouchable. When God's Word is flowing through you, you become His conduit. The Word is like a repellent to your enemies. If someone speaks against you or rises up against you, they speak against the One who is resident within you. This is why Peter said to Ananias, "You have not lied to me, but to Holy Spirit..." On a side note: be careful how you answer your man or woman of God; they are the oracles of God's Word for your life.

When you pray God's Word, you are praying directly to the author! His Word supersedes your will, your wants and your disappointments. You must allow His Word to supersede your will, your desires, your work schedule, your personal needs, your dreams and wishes because His will is done. When we ask God for a miracle, He gives us a directive. It is not up for discussion; it is not open for compromise; it is not something you can do half way. This is the part of prayer that many believers have difficulty with because they do not follow through. If God's instruction is to dip in the Jordan River 7 times, but you only dip 3 times, do not be surprised when you do not receive what you asked for! The proper protocol to prayer is really asking for instruction, not so much for the answer. When we follow the instruction given, we ignite the Word that God has already spoken over our situation, and then, we see the full manifestation of what we prayed.

I'm afraid that some erroneous interpretations of the authority of the believer have led many to mouthing off rather than declaring an effective, fervent prayer that avails much. Even Christ had to align himself with the laws of the Father. If this were not so, why would the Father instruct him to submit to John the Baptist to receive baptism? If his divinity was all he needed, the baptism would not have been necessary. Even Christ was subject to the protocol and instruction of the Father. Christ was human and referred to himself as the Son of Man. The humanity of Christ required that he submit to the protocol of the Father.

John 14:28 (NIV) You heard me say I am going away and I am coming back to you. If you loved me, you would be glad that I am going to the Father, for the Father is greater than I. Christ is subject to the Father and seated at His right hand making intercession for us all. Christ did not come to abolish the law, but to fulfill it. The first and only required human sacrifice among the Jews occurred when Christ aligned himself with the protocol of His Father. Christ, the Firstfruit of many, was obedient even unto death. By his obedience, he became the seed that brought forth the New Covenant paving the way for us to become the Sons of God.

Jeremiah 31:33-34 (KJV) "This is the covenant I will make with the house of Israel after that time," declares the LORD. "I will put my law in their minds and write it on their hearts. I will be their God and they will be my people. No longer will a man teach his neighbor, or a man his brother, saying 'Know the LORD,' because they will all know me, from the least of them to the greatest." declares the LORD. Hebrews 8:10 (AMP) For this is the covenant that I will make with the house of Israel After those days, says the Lord: I will imprint My laws upon their minds [even upon their innermost thoughts and understanding], And engrave them upon their hearts [effecting their regeneration]. And I will be their God, And they shall be My people.

It has been discovered that people who are religiously inclined have something that is measurably different in the design and makeup of their brains. God has written His laws, His Word in our hearts and minds! American molecular geneticist, Dr. Dean Hamer, has concluded after comparing more than 2,000 DNA samples that a person's capacity to believe in God is linked to brain chemicals. "Religious believers can point to the existence of God genes as one more sign of the Creator's ingenuity — a clever way to help humans acknowledge and embrace a divine presence."

CHAPTER SEVEN
WHAT'S IN A NAME?

God is not a man that He could ever lie. And when He says something is about to happen, you can rest assured it is going to happen! He moves sovereignly by His own Word, and He backs it up by His name. He sealed His Word with His own name, His signature. The word *name* means authority, character and honor.

WISDOM PRINCIPLE: YOU CAN ONLY BELIEVE GOD'S WORD TO THE EXTENT THAT YOU BELIEVE IN HIS NAME.

For too long, Christians have been comfortable accepting the name of God as simply a three-letter word ascribed to a deity. Unfortunately, Allah's followers call their god, *'god'* as well. Buddhist's worshipers call their Buddha, god, and every other religion refers to their god as god. Can we agree that surely our God has a name above all other names? Can we agree that our God cares very much about His name because His Word is filled with instruction on speaking His most Holy Name. The Bible also commands that we give honor to *the* name, to worship *the* name, to revere *the* name... Obviously, there is a differentiating factor between our God and all other gods. He desires that His people have spiritual comprehension regarding His name and how He feels about it. Oftentimes, we refer to Him simply as Lord, which means captain, Adonai, Elohim, and many of the other well-intended titles man has ascribed to the Almighty. However, without His name, He really does not have a true identity, and we cannot appreciate His character, honor and authority.

You can speak the Word, but you will not be able to access the full power without knowing and believing in the name of the God of Abraham, Isaac and Jacob. Remember, the word *name* means character, honor, and authority. A person's word is invalid without his/her name. A testimony is inadmissible without the honor and authority of the character witness. Thus, the authority of the believer is found in the power of the name of the Most High God. This book would be pointless without the understanding and revelation of the true name of the true God.

What is His name? You're probably thinking, you already know His name because you are a Christian; and as a Christian, we are taught that God's name is Jesus. And nothing could be further from the truth. There is so much that has been lost to transliteration, which is why I wrote this book on the LORD'S Prayer based on the ancient Aramaic translation.

The first thing you must understand is that Jesus/Yahshua is a transliteration of a Hebrew name Yeshua or Joshua, just as Moses is a transliteration of the Egyptian name Munius, which the Torah translates into Hebrew as Moshe or Moses. In fact, Joshua and Jesus are the same name! And yet, we know and understand that there is a vast difference between these two names and certainly these two great figures in Scripture. Notwithstanding, they are both powerful. However, only one carries the most Holy Name given by the Father. I am not going to delve too deeply into this topic because it deserves an entire book of its own, of which I already have a manuscript and is now a work in progress entitled The Most Holy Name.

It is vitally important that we understand the power of a name. I sat here in my study pondering whether or not to include this chapter because it may come across controversial, but then again, this whole book is filled with controversy much like when Jesus/Yahshua stood before the Pharisees and Sadducees, and they questioned His motives, His actions and His teachings. Nevertheless, when confronted with a perfect storm, there is great need for fresh revelation to get you through the storm.

What's in a name? Everyone goes through seasons in life where your name changes according to your age. As a child I was known as Tommy. In Middle School, I accidentally went by my given name, Thomas, because one of my teachers called out for Thomas during the roll call, and I answered. Everyone immediately adapted to the name. When I married, my wife and I were known as Tom and Judy because one of our pastor's wives called us Tom and Judy, and one of the daughters called each of us Tom-and-Judy. We were each Tom-and-Judy. When I wrote my first book, The Agreement, I became Dr. Thomas Michael. ...but what about when your name gets dragged through the mud? When your credibility is questioned, it is more than your ego that gets bruised; it is your character that comes into question. When your name becomes associated with negative circumstances whether true or false, it loses integrity with some people and no longer carries the same weight. This is the time to make an exchange with God. Just as with Jesus/Yahshua, He will give His name in exchange for yours. His name has power; His name has authority; His name has honor and represents the character of who He is!

Several years ago, I went through a very difficult time in my ministry. Some people left our church and began spreading false rumors about our church and about me. They went to the media with false allegations in the hopes of shutting our church and ministry down. It was not long before my name had been drug through the muck and the mire of a biased, slanted, prejudiced media. Roberts Liardon, an evangelist from California, was scheduled to minister at our church and delivered a message about the fact that our names cannot save, heal, or deliver anyone! I realized at that moment the importance and value of the most Holy Name of God, the same name He bestowed upon His Son, Christ. I quickly realized that my name means nothing if I don't truly know His name. I began my quest for finding out His name instead of just His title as a deity. For years, I wondered what the word Jah in my King James Bible meant.

(In some translations it appears as Jah and in others YAH.)

Psalm 68:4 (NKJV) Sing to God, sing praises to His name; Extol Him who rides on the clouds, By His name YAH, And rejoice before Him. I researched and discovered the last letter in the English language to be added to the alphabet was the letter 'J'. I began to understand the influence that translation and transliteration has had upon the Scriptures, not to mention the Most Holy Name. After realizing that this YAH was part of God's root name, I stumbled upon an even greater enigmatic surprise. I realized that God had hidden the root part of His Most Holy Name in the majority of the prophets' names! JeremiYAH, HezekiYAH, ZephaniYAH, ObediYAH, ZechariYAH and so many others. About the same time I made this discovery, I was working on a sermon using a very high tech computer Bible and concordance researching the few places where the name YAH/JAH showed up. I decided to click on the YAH; and lo and behold, the computer began speaking to me! I was literally dumbfounded! All the other words with tags simply redirected to me to text concerning the names in question. This time, the designer of the software had added audible voicing, and the voice began to expound on this YAH being part of the Most Holy Name of the Hebrew and Christian God. It went on to confirm some findings about the Tetragrammaton. I was excited to learn that this was and is the original, untouched, uncensored name of the Most High! YHVH is His name! I am sure you have probably heard of the transliteration of this name into YEHOVAH or JEHOVAH. In the Hebrew text, there were no vowels, which gives this Most Holy Name an even greater connection with the supernatural because it was customary to add breath in the place of vowels to pronounce the Hebrew words. During the process of transliterations, the name went from YHVH to YEHOVAH to JEHOVAH, and the other name most Christians are familiar with—YAHWEH or YAHVEH. (Remember that the letters "W" and "V" are often reversed as in the German language, i.e., Volkswagen is pronounced *Wolksvagen* in German.)

It really is exciting to see how this Most Holy Name connects Jesus/Yahshua to the Father in a greater way than our English translation. The root word for Jesus/Yahshua's name in Hebrew is *Yah*, which means God and *shuah* meaning who saves. YAHVEH means God of covenant. "Hallelujah," or better yet "HalleluYAH," is a universal word, which sounds the same in every language, from Hebrew to Manderin Chinese, to Spanish. It actually means, "We *must* praise YAH!" Do you remember sitting around a campfire when you were young and singing a little song that went like this? "KumbaYAH, my LORD, KumbaYAH, Oh LORD, KumbaYAH." It literally means, come by here my LORD, come by here... God's Most Holy Name has been hidden smack dab in the middle of our lives, and we didn't even realize it! I am sure you are thinking that the only name you need is Jesus, and I couldn't agree with you more. However, Jesus is one of the most poorly transliterated names of all time! The name Jesus comes from the name Iesous, which is a translation from the Hebrew name Yeshua or Yahshua. As Christians, we are taught to pray in the name of Jesus, so one day when I finished praying and closed out my prayer, I said, "In the most holy name of Yahshua Ha-Mashiach, and all of a sudden, another revelation became clearer! When the Bible says, "There is healing *'in'* the name of YAHshua." It became very clear to me, the healing part is in the YAH part because it is the root part of the name of YAHVEH. It is obvious that the Joshua part of the name has no more power than my name, Thomas, even though it was one of the apostles' names. The power is in the YAH part of the name of Jesus/Yahshua. There's healing *in* (YAH) the Name! The healing is hidden in the YAH part of the name of *Yah*shua! Nevertheless, I understand when people still use the name Jesus because we have grown to love that name. Even in its transliterated state, it can raise the dead!

It is quite normal to have an attachment to the name of Jesus. I do believe that there is power in the name of Jesus even though it's a transliteration. I believe God can heal people in the name of Jesus. I believe we can be saved through the name of Jesus. But why not call him by His real name? The authority is in the official name. It is like when a child grows up hearing his/her parents calling each other honey or dear; the child eventually picks up the idea that the parent's name is Honey or Dear. It is not until they are *mature* enough to understand the difference and produce a sentence. However, the doting parent responds to the child's every call and answers to any name.

Let's say you know a wealthy man named Bob, who has

bequeathed all of his riches to you, but if you try to access his money, the name Bob holds no power of attorney. It's not until you use the name Robert that you gain access to all that he has. You may have had access to his wealth while he was alive, and you called him Bob, Bobby or Uncle B. But now that he is gone, you must use his proper, given name to access all that he has bequeathed to you!

Abram and Sarai received a name change by adding just one letter from the Tetragrammaton (the four letter name of God, YHVH). God added the letter H or Hei in Hebrew to their names, and they were transformed! Abram became Abraham and Sarai became Sarah. The name Abram means exalted father, whilst, Abraham means "father of a multitude" or "chief of multitude," friend of God. Abraham, by God's elective covenant, became the founder of the Hebrew nation. Abram did well as an "exalted father", but his name transformed him into God's friend, who is the father of many. God was, essentially, engrafting His initials into the lives of Abraham and Sarah! Sarai means princess or noble lady and she became Sarah, wife of Abraham and mother of Jacob. Do not hesitate for a moment and think Sarah got less than Abraham. Her offspring was connected to the lineage of Yahshua. What's in a name?

Let me close out this chapter with an epiphany I had a couple of years ago. Our modern age has given light to so many of the world's religions. Since the advent of the Internet, we have been made more aware of all the different cultures and religions of the world. I have heard commentators and philosophers refer to the *three main* religions of the world: Judaism, Christianity and Islam. I know that Muslims call their god, Allah and that Jews call their God, YHVH, but then I became a bit perplexed because Christianity seemingly has two names! God and Jesus! Although we are taught that they are one and the same, I have also recognized that the Godhead consists of three, Who are in such complete covenant/agreement with each other that They are One. Scripture substantiates, in both Old Testament and New Testament, that there is only *one* Ha-Shem/Name. And that name is above every name on earth! This led me to a series of questions that led me down the path of the Most Holy Name, the Most Holy Vehement Name of God. My search led me to my Jewish ancestral roots, and I quickly realized that God, in His infinite wisdom, had predestined everything I was feeling and thinking because I am privileged to be a part of His chosen people. Being Jewish, I sensed a strong connection to the God of Abraham, Isaac and Jacob; and yet, I seldom heard anyone mention His name. My ancestors were forbidden to speak the Most Holy Name for fear of blasphemy, and I did not know too many people in my Christian upbringing that ever referred to God by his Most Holy Name—YHVH or YAHVEH. Yet, Judeo/Christianity had morphed from this same God, whose name had been obscured for centuries. So, if Christianity comes from the Old Testament God, who foretold of the coming of the Messiah, the Son of the Most High God, how could there be two holy names?

After my mother's conversion to Christianity, I grew up a good ole' Southern Baptist boy and was taught from an early age to pray in the most holy name of Jesus. I experienced good things by the power of the name of the son of the Most High God. The name, Jesus, was rooted deeply in my spiritual journey and was strongly entrenched in my mind. It's funny because even my surname suffered an identity crisis before I was ever even born. My ancestors are Sephardic Jews and came to the Americas from Spain. My father's ancestors arrived here with a different name than what we have now. What's in a name? In this case, it was life saving to my great grandparents who, no doubt, fled Spain under less than fortunate circumstances.

Christianity, Islam and Judaism have their origins in the same region of the world. They are rooted in Abraham's lineage and foundation. The thing that sets these religions apart from every other religion is their claim to theism or the belief that there is only one god. If I am not mistaken, most of the other religions have multiple deities. Nevertheless, that is not as important as the fact that these three religions have their own god. In fact, the Arabic word, Allah actually means god.

What's in a name? Could this "name" issue be a game-changer in our prayers? The word "name" means character, honor and authority. Without character, you cannot have honor, and without honor, you cannot have authority. A man who pushes his weight around has no true lasting authority. Soon, there will be someone stronger to bring him down. He may force someone to do what he wants for the moment, but when the individual tires of oppression, he will leave him. The oppressor has no real authority because he has no honor. The authority of the believer, as has been taught for many years, is not based on the scriptures alone, but on the One who backs every word by His name.

Psalm 138:2 (NASB) I will bow down toward Your holy temple And give thanks to Your name for Your lovingkindness and Your truth; For You have magnified Your word according to all Your name. The Scripture states very clearly that it is the traditions of men, which make the word of God ineffective. Unfortunately, our westernized Judeo/Christian faith has suffered at the hands of the *traditions* of men. The greatest travesty that ever happened to religion is the separation of Judaism and Christianity. It is no secret that Jesus/Yahshua was a Jew, as was Paul and the other disciples. They were practicing Jews who kept the laws and the feasts of YAHVEH. The Christ of Christianity was and is a Jew; he was educated in the synagogues and temples of the day. He is part of the chosen race: God's people. This same Christ is the Messiah that had been promised to the Jews, who would come from the Jewish lineage of King David. I hope you are beginning to see the historical background of the Most Holy Name and the importance of using this Most Holy Name to access all that God/YAHVEH has for us!

Psalm 119:165 (KJV) Great peace have they which love thy law: and nothing shall offend them. I pray that you are not offended with any of the revelations in this book because the only thing I am trying to do is help you unlock the vaults of heaven. "Uncle Bobby" can do a lot to help you while he is here with you, but when he goes away, it is only his power of attorney connected to his full name that will allow you access to his assets. You have now been given the power of attorney to act in his absence. When Jesus/Yahshua died on Calvary, it was for more than just redemption from the power of sin over your life. It was so you could have life and have it more abundantly! He has given you power of attorney through his last will and *testament*. All of the Old and New Testaments promises are yours!

My sound engineer of many years shared an experience he had during a family reunion. He traveled to his hometown for the reunion and was in Sunday service at the church where he grew up.

As he sat in the "old time religion" atmosphere he realized the people were still the same as they had been when he lived there 20 years prior! He said it was as though the people were frozen in time with the same ideals and a poverty mentality. He realized how successful he was spiritually, emotionally and economically and felt he had grown much under the covering of our church. There is so much we can miss if we are not open to revelation and do not progress with the leading of Holy Spirit. The Bible says it is Holy Spirit who will lead you into *all* truth.

The Psalmist, David, wrote, "One thing have I desired of the LORD..." What a simple request from the one whom the Bible says was a man after God's own heart. Out of all that King David had at his disposal, he only desired *one thing*. One thing! That is both amazing to me and startling. Although, when I look at it from the grand scheme of things, I fully understand his request. One thing—to be in His presence. There is power in oneness and singularity. It provides an acute focus zeroed in on its target. The Bible is clear about certain singularities such as ONE God, ONE Spirit, ONE Savior, ONE LORD, ONE baptism, ONE church, and ONE chosen people! There is power in the ONE name of YAH. Yahshua was chosen to be the only begotten son. Begotten means to bear, to bring forth; used metaphorically of causing or engendering moral and spiritual relations and states of the new birth in the Holy Spirit. Men, who obey and love God as sons are begotten of Him.

Yahshua criticized the eloquent prayers of the Pharisees and Sadducees because they were lofty, and presumptuous. When we use prayer as a wish list, it is presumptuous of us because God has already purposed to bless us in every way possible.

I sat in a conference in Columbus, Georgia with many educated men and women belonging to a Christian university of which I was the youngest professor. People, whose time had come and some whose time had passed them by, surrounded me. I don't mean to sound selective, but there is a season to everything. I was honored and ever grateful being in such a great cloud of witnesses. I leaned back in my chair as the professorial show of who had more degrees, more books, bigger churches, greater ministries, etc., etc. paraded before me. I heard Holy Spirit whisper, "I want to give you all the desires of your heart, so that you desire nothing else, but me."

As a result, I penned down the words to a beautiful worship song that stirs me deep within my spirit and gives me singularity of purpose and singularity of worship.

WHO HAVE I TO DESIRE, BUT THEE?
WHO HAVE I TO DEFEND ME, BUT THEE?
ONLY YOU CAN SATISFY MY SOUL,
ONLY YOU CAN SATISFY AND EXCEED MY EVERY GOAL.
ONLY YOU CAN DO EXCEEDINGLY, ABUNDANTLY ABOVE
ALL I ASK FOR.
WHO HAVE I TO DESIRE, BUT THEE?

In the end, like Jesus/Yahshua who is one with the Father and desires nothing more than to be with and in the Father, we too have nothing more to desire, but His presence. Something supernatural happens when you come into oneness, into singularity with God— you and the Father: one heart, one mind, one spirit... Too often, believers enter into a duplicitous mindset about the character and nature of God because of the confused roles of the Godhead that religion has by imagery painted in our hearts and minds. The book of James tells us a double minded man is unstable in all his ways. David wrote in Psalm 119:9-11 (AMP) How can a young man keep his way pure? By keeping watch [on himself] according to Your word [conforming his life to Your precepts]. With all my heart I have sought You, [inquiring of You and longing for You]; Do not let me wander from Your commandments [neither through ignorance nor by willful disobedience]. Your word I have treasured *and* stored in my heart, That I may not sin against You. Blessed and reverently praised are You, O Lord; Teach me Your statutes.

In this passage, the term *word* is used in verse nine, and then, again in verse eleven. In verse nine, the term comes from the Hebrew word "dabar" which means by implication, matter, a cause, act or advice, affair. In verse eleven, the term *word* is from the Hebrew word "amar", a primitive root that means the answer, speech and *name*. Did you catch that? His Word is His name and His name is His Word! The Word of God has power on two levels, because truth is parallel. It is like a two-edged sword!

To know His Word and His name is to know His character, honor and authority. If you know His Word, you know His character because they are synonymous. There are many Christians who can quote Scripture, but they live impoverished lives and are always sickly. It takes more than just knowing and even speaking His Word, you must follow the directives of Holy Spirit who leads us into all truth. Namaan was directed to submerge himself in the Jordan River seven times to be cured of leprosy. When we ask God for a miracle, He gives us a directive! A directive is more than a simple instruction. Directives must be followed without question and instructions can be optional. Have you ever purchased an item that required assembly? The instructions are strictly optional! You can build the thing without instructions, but you may end up with left over nuts and bolts, which could eventually compromise the integrity of the item. However, if you were building the Empire State Building in New York, you would have to follow every detail of the plans otherwise the structural integrity of the building could be compromised. You must follow the directives of His instruction!

WISDOM PRINCIPLE: WHEN YOU ASK GOD FOR A ANYTHING, HE WILL GIVE YOU A DIRECTIVE.

His Word is His Name and His Name is His Word!

CHAPTER EIGHT
RENUNCIATION OF YOUR WILL

We are living in the age of the selfie. I have to admit I have taken a few selfies myself, but I am convinced, we have opened up a Pandora's box. I have no problem with social media, and I enjoy reading peoples' posts and watching their crazy video antics. But I have become quite concerned at the self-absorption mindset that is slowly creeping into the hearts of believers. All the self-talk about being the best and "bleep this" and "bleep that" proves that people are becoming more and more narcissistic. I heard a news commentator speak of a new politician who displayed all the symptoms and characteristics of NPD or narcissistic personality disorder. And yet, many people are looking to this politician for answers!

Many people leave their purpose and calling to search out their career and dream, citing their unhappiness as reason enough to uproot and move across country. There are times when we are going to be called to do things where we are not happy. The Bible does not say, "The happiness of the LORD is my strength." "The joy of the LORD is my strength." It's the *joy* of the LORD that gets you through those times when you don't *feel happy,* and you feel unfulfilled. You will only find joy when you choose to do God's will over your own.

I don t believe you can actually enter into the fullness of God's blessings until you have renounced your own will and any other ideals, whether they be secular or religious. Just because The Perfect Prayer says "His will is done..." does not mean He will push and bully His way into your life. God wants to be chosen. God wants to be loved. God wants to be worshiped and adored. He wants us to make Him a part of our daily wants, needs, desires, wishes and dreams. God wants you to choose Him above all other gods.

WISDOM PRINCIPLE: ANYTHING THAT COMPETES WITH YOUR AFFECTION FOR THE FATHER HAS THE POTENTIAL OF BECOMING AN IDOL.

You must be willing to bring down the idols in your life. You cannot pray them away; you cannot wish them away. They are not going to go away on their own. You must cut down the idols with the sword of the Spirit, which is the Word of God.

God knows we are creatures of habit. He wants us to create rituals, habits or patterns that will keep us on a faithful regimen of worship. Everyone is ritualistic about certain things in their lives. Don't you wake up each morning and begin a daily routine: brushing your teeth, showering, getting dressed for the day? Why is it that many Christians have a difficult time when it comes to ritualism concerning their relationship with the LORD? You are not always yielded to His will, even if you pray daily. What you see, feel, taste, touch and hear moves you; therefore, you are probably praying according to your will and not His will. **There must be a shifting of power and authority from self to God.**

This is where the prayer, ritual or pattern of renunciation comes into play. Rituals are an intrinsic part of our mental, emotional and spiritual makeup. These unseen patterns create paths that keep us on or off of the track of righteousness. They create paths that lead to God's abundance or lack. We must create patterns that will lead us straight to Him; otherwise, we will be destined to follow the addictive patterns of this world. Remember the adage, "Like father, like son"? An abusive father often produces an abusive son. The Perfect Prayer aligns you with God's perfect will; now we're ready for the adage, "Like Father, Like Son." We pray, not for things, but to be more like Him. When my beautiful daughter Katherine was two years old she brilliantly explained to a room full of people, "I look like my mommy, but I'm just like my daddy cause I spit!" She had watched me spit while I was working in the yard outdoors.

I was flipping through channels the other day and ran across a preacher who was preaching on the subject of prayer. He was telling his audience that he did not want someone praying for him who would simply ask for God's will to be done. He said, "If I am dying, I want someone that prays me back to life!" I could understand his motives; I could not understand his ignorance! Did you catch that? He said, "I don't want anyone praying God's will." What makes us think we can pray anything, *but* God's perfect will? Did you answer in your head – arrogance? Exactly! That's not faith; that's sheer ignorance founded on arrogance. We have to break these patterns to move forward! The only way to break through the worldly rituals or patterns in your life is to connect with the supernatural where these negative patterns can be renounced and are subject to the ONE TRUE GOD: YAHVEH.

A few weeks ago, I distinctly heard Holy Spirit say, "I am here to interrupt your patterns." For the next several weeks, I taught on the topic of interrupting patterns. Joseph, a young nine-year-old boy in our church, was sitting in the car with his mother and grandmother after Sunday service. The mom was resisting the popular family vote of where to eat, wherein with his most serious face and much conviction, he looked at his mother and said, "Mom, change your patterns." We have to be willing to change our patterns and adapt to the patterns of the ancient wisdom of the Bible that has been proven for generations! Revelations from Scripture are really not revelations because they've been there all along. It's like the story that was in the news the other day about a family who had lived in a home for some time. When finally, they decided to clean out the attic, I'm not sure if they were packing up to move else where, nevertheless, they came across a painting. They decided to have it checked. Turns out, it was a Rembrandt or some famous artwork that was worth over one million dollars! I'm ready for Holy Spirit to interrupt my patterns and show me something that is already there, but I cannot yet see it.

1 Kings 19:1-7 (NIV) Now Ahab told Jezebel everything Elijah had done and how he had killed all the prophets with the sword. So Jezebel sent a messenger to Elijah to say, "May the gods deal with me, be it ever so severely, if by this time tomorrow I do not make your life like that of one of them." Elijah was afraid and ran for his life. When he came to Beersheba in Judah, he left his servant there, while he himself went a day's journey into the wilderness. He came to a broom bush, sat down under it and prayed that he might die. "I have had enough, Lord," he said. "Take my life; I am no better than my ancestors." Then he lay down under the bush and fell asleep. All at once an angel touched him and said, *"Get up and eat."* He looked around, and there by his head was some bread baked over hot coals, and a jar of water. He ate and drank and then lay down again. The angel of the Lord came back a second time and touched him and said, "Get up and eat, for the journey is too much for you."

This was a time of drought; and subsequently, a time of famine would soon follow. I remember a couple of families in our church who were so worried about the Y2K scare that they stocked up on a years supply of canned goods and had cases of water stacked high because they believed the media hype. They should have shown a little confidence in me as their man of God because I shared from the pulpit that God had given me a word that everything was going to be OK. They would have saved thousands of dollars had they listened to the man of God instead of the fear-filled news. Sadly, a few years later this precious family left our church. Not because of the Y2K scam, but because the patterns and habits of rebellion to God's authority were deeply rooted in them. People do what they do, usually because they don't want anyone telling them what to do. Old habits die hard.

When people think a catastrophe is imminent, they tend to act crazy and forget that God should be our source in every situation come what may. God is our source in the good times and the bad. Many people horde when they are fearful of lack, but look at the young prophet-to-be, Elisha, he sowed in a time of famine! I believe part of the reason he was chosen was his faith! He was plowing the fallow ground with 12 plows! Most people would have given up and held on to their plows and oxen because that is the natural tendency when it comes to the fear of lack.

I recently read a post by someone on Facebook where T.D. Jakes was quoted saying that the famine was over. I immediately claimed it for my household, myself and for our church. I was so excited because it seemed like a confirmation by a very popular celebrity-preacher, and it coincided with the famine that I had been talking about for weeks. Then I heard Holy Spirit say, "The famine is not over. The *drought* is over." I thought to myself, well that's the same thing isn't it? Holy Spirit showed me first, the rain comes after the drought and waters the earth; then, the sower sows the seed. A few months later the harvest is ready! I got excited over the harvest, and Holy Spirit then said, "After the harvest comes harvesting!" *Then,* the famine is over! We want to jump right to the famine-is-over, when there are several natural steps of obedience that must be adhered before you reap. Before the famine is over in your life, you must understand the progress. The rain must come first; then you sow, then you wait, and finally comes the harvesting. Only after the harvesting will the famine over! A lot of people think that sowing seed and waiting for the harvest is hard, but the real hard work for the farmer is the harvesting. Sowing seeds involves simply dropping the seeds into the ground and trusting that they will produce a harvest. Then, when they grow and produce their fruit, you have to go out and pick the fruit. The tough part is harvesting all the blessings. But that's proof the famine is over. Now, it's time to enjoy the bounty.

At one point in Elijah's life God was feeding him with food the ravens brought to him. God makes provision for us, enough so that we don't die during the famine, but it is not an abundant harvest yet! God is a gracious God, and He looks out for us even when we are full of ourselves and are operating by our own ego. This is why we must come to the place where we renounce our own will, our own desires and embrace the will of the Father. "Our Heavenly Father. Hallowed is Thy Name. Your Kingdom is come, Your will *is* done..." What did Jesus/Yahshua pray in the Garden of Gethsemane? He did not say, "LORD, I want to serve you and love you, but on my terms. I will go to Calvary, but I want nothing to do with crosses and crowns of thorns..." No! He said, "Nevertheless, not my will, but thy will *is* done." He renounced his own will and embraced the will of the Father, and thereby, brought about salvation for the world.

At one point, Elijah was in the throws of depression, exhaustion, disillusionment and his I-want-to-give-up state of mind. He was being affected by his emotions, and his love and commitment to the LORD came into question. I am sure we can all relate, but he had to move past his feelings and deny his own will.

1 Kings 19:8-9 (NIV) So he got up and ate and drank. Strengthened by that food, he traveled forty days and forty nights until he reached Horeb, the mountain of God. There he went into a cave and spent the night. Did you hear that? You have to move past your emotions, your ego, your quitting stage. It's not an attack from the devil; it's YOU! You have the power over your destiny, and only you can activate the will of God for your life. Get up!

Elijah got up and ate and journeyed to the next phase of his life and had an encounter with God. God will do the same for any of His children. Just because you are going through a difficult time in your life does not mean the devil has gotten the best of you. Some Christians think that they are better than others because they are in a time of harvesting when someone else is in a time of drought and famine. God has sent me as the messenger to interrupt your patterns and habits! Get up! Get excited! If you have sown a seed, it is a signal to God to schedule your harvests. Your famine will soon be over!

WISDOM PRINCIPLE: YOUR SEED SENDS A SIGNAL TO GOD TO SCHEDULE A HARVEST.

Ecclesiastes 11:4 (CJB) He who keeps watching the wind will never sow; he who keeps looking at the clouds will never reap. The reason some peoples' famines last longer is because they failed to sow *in* the time of drought. They're looking at their circumstances, and like the couple in our church who horded during the Y2K season, they are moved by the fearful news they hear. The famine in Elijah's day was not over until the drought was first over, and it was Elijah himself who was holding back the rain. Remember when Elijah said, I Kings 17:1 (NIV) ...As surely as the LORD, the

God of Israel, lives—the God I serve—there will be no dew or rain during the next few years until I give the word!

And yet, some people would rather starve than to bless a prophet. Sowing a seed to a man of God could end their drought, but many walk in fear because of the famine. Elijah may have become discouraged because no one was willing to sow into his life during the famine, when all the while he, the prophet who stopped the rain, had the power to call forth rain! One action affects another's action. God is here to interrupt our patterns!

He's interrupting your patterns. You cannot be moved by what you see, feel, taste, touch or hear. I am speaking to your heart: your subconscious mind. Because all the things around you are temporal! Your car is temporal! Your house is temporal! Your furniture is temporal! You must renounce your own will and embrace the will of the Father.

Why do we allow these THINGS to govern how we feel? Emotions are nothing more than the way we think about the things we experience. Why do married people split up? Because someone allowed their emotions and their ego to dictate how they feel, and subsequently, they end up in the desert of matrimony feeling unloved. If they were so in love, how can they fall out of love? Because their patterns have been set by their thoughts and interpretation of love, and these affect what they *feel*. These thought patterns, or self-talk, form the foundation of emotional experience. Your self-talk will reflect whatever environmental, biological or physiological factors are influencing your feelings. Change your mental pattern, and you change your emotion. Mental patterns flow like rivers, but the water in the river has no control over where it flows.

Elijah was *the* prophet of God. He was the anointed, appointed miracle worker; and yet, he was at a place where he wanted to die. They didn't make Prozac and mood altering drugs back then. He had to allow the LORD to interrupt the patterns of his life. But Elijah had to make the first move. God will meet you were you are, but you must be willing to do something you've never done to have something you've never had.

The purpose of this book is to return your will to God's will and place your entire trust and life in His hands. The ultimate, perfect will of God emerges in the abandonment of self and complete capitulation of your will into His will. I purposely used the word capitulation because it means to declare defeat. Many believers are accustomed to the use of the word surrender that causes them to be mentally incapable of fully grasping what surrendering truly calls for. Think about the last Holy Ghost-filled, God-encounter service you were in: people falling on their faces, people crying, preachers prophesying and emotions running the gamut. When it was over, most remained unchanged, perhaps, including you! Are you still behaving the same? Are you still dealing with the same feelings and motives about past relationships? Are you still holding aught against a former pastor? Are you still holding on to unresolved issues with your past and still dealing with the same habitual sins?

You must be willing to embrace and accept where you are NOW, and know that when you align with God's perfect will, everything will change. You will change! Your household will change! Because you are no longer living in the past or dreaming about the future, instead you are embracing your NOW. Quit trying to have faith for something you don't even know how to handle. God's will is in the NOW. He is a right-now God! Now faith is…

If you declare Christ as the victorious savior, then, you must be the one who capitulated. God's Word says, "In our weakness, He is made strong." This is hard for the selfie-generation and the faith-generation to accept because the selfie-generation is constantly declaring how wonderful we are and the faith-generation is always declaring how victorious we are. I'm all for calling those things, which be not as though they were, but not to the point of self-delusion. You can't be more than a conqueror until you first renounce your will and embrace His will and move into His perfect purpose. Then, you qualify to be called more than a conqueror! More than a conqueror comes when you enter into His perfect will. You cannot get to that place of victory until you get your stubborn will out of the way. It is not your declaration that makes you more than a conqueror. The Word of God releases the power to declare that you are more than a conqueror. You must move into the realm of the unseen to undo the negative patterns and renounce your will. The process begins with giving and receiving forgiveness.

One of the most debatable issues in Christendom has to do with forgiving sins. The Catholic Church believes that priests have the authority, by God, to absolve sins. Like the old hymn goes,

"What can wash away my sins? Nothing but the blood of Jesus/Yahshua." Yet, there are scriptures that are easily interpreted to give the believer the power to remit sin as in John 20:23. In the Greek, the first verbs are in the aorist verb tense and the second verbs are in the perfect tense. The perfect tense implies an abiding state that commenced before the action of the aorist tense. Literally, the text is saying, "Those whose sins you forgive have already been forgiven; those whose sins you do not forgive, have not already been forgiven." This means the apostles, and those after them, were only authorized to declare forgiveness consistent with what the LORD had already determined was forgiven. On the day of Pentecost, guided by Holy Spirit, the apostles did not personally forgive anyone's sins; they merely announced the conditions of pardon that men and women were acquiescent to. To forgive actually means to release. We may not be able to forgive someone who has hurt us, but we certainly can release him or her. In the traditional LORD'S Prayer, Catholic doctrine teaches, "forgive us our trespasses as we forgive those who trespass against us..." while some Protestant churches have opted for, "forgive us our debts as we forgive our debtors..." as is found in the English Standard Version Bible. In other words "Forgive my trespasses/debts to the degree that I forgive others." If salvation hinges on forgiveness and if God forgives us, whether trespass or debt according to how we forgive, we are all doomed! There is probably a person in your life, whether consciously or unconsciously, you have failed to forgive. We are forgiven because of Christ's redemptive work at Calvary. Interestingly enough, in the original Aramaic translation, there is no argument because it does not deal with how we forgive, but rather, serenity. "...and leave us serene, just as we allowed others serenity." Serenity is all about finding your peace and remaining in it. God's will always brings peace. Jesus/Yahshua was wrought with anguish in the Garden of Gethsemane until he said, "Nevertheless, not my will, but your will be done," and suddenly he was able to cope with the cross that was set before Him and His serenity was restored. He entered a state of serenity and took upon Himself the sins of the world. Serenity is about not offending others and allowing them to remain in their peace, thus walking in serenity yourself. Perhaps, this is the secret behind the success so many have had with the Alcoholics Anonymous organizations. In AA meetings you are taught to change what you can and accept what you cannot change and pray for wisdom to know the difference.

John 20:19 (KJV) Then the same day at evening, being the first day of the week, when the doors were shut where the disciples were assembled for fear of the Jews, came Jesus/Yahshua and stood in the midst, and saith unto them, "Peace." The word *peace*, not only means quietness and prosperity, but it actually means to set at *one* again, to put back together. That is serenity! When we are undone by chaos, hurt, and trauma, we tend to fall apart, but we can be put back together again. Christ had to put the disciples back together again because they were undone when they beheld his miraculous presence. He was once dead; and now, he was alive. He showed up unannounced in a room with locked doors. He had transitioned into a spiritual dimension that allowed him access to move through solid matter. Quantum physics supports this phenomenon. The idea that matter can break down into small molecular parts allowing it to pass through solid matter, and then reassemble into its original state can only happen in God's dimension and power. Talk about interrupting patterns! He interrupted everything they had ever known historically and spiritually. He not only was "once dead" and now "was alive," but he moved in a different dimension that allowed him access into a fortified locked room.

John 20:20 (KJV) And when he had so said, he shewed unto them his hands and his side. Then were the disciples glad, when they saw the Lord. They did not recognize the Lord until they saw the proof of the crucifixion in his hands and feet. Their eyes had been emblazoned by the bloody image of his body on the cross at Calvary where they had last seen him. Their will, their emotions, their thoughts, their beliefs had been conformed to what they had experienced instead of the power and authority they had come to know in the Messiah when they walked with him. So, Jesus/Yahshua had to declare peace over them again. He had to bring them back together again and realign their thoughts.

Verse 21-29 Then said Jesus/Yahshua to them again, Peace be unto you: as my Father hath sent me, even so send I you. And when he had said this, he breathed on them, and saith unto them, Receive ye the Holy Ghost: Whose soever sins ye remit, they are remitted unto them; and whose soever sins ye retain, they are retained. But Thomas, one of the twelve, called Didymus, was not with them when Jesus/Yahshua came. The other disciples therefore said unto him, We have seen the Lord. But he said unto them, Except I shall see in his hands the print of the nails, and put my finger into the print of the nails, and thrust my hand into his side, I will not believe. And after eight days again his disciples were within, and Thomas with them: then came Jesus/Yahshua, the doors being shut, and stood in the midst, and said, Peace be unto you. Then saith he to Thomas, Reach hither thy finger, and behold my hands; and reach hither thy hand, and thrust it into my side: and be not faithless, but believing. And Thomas answered and said unto him, My Lord and my God. Jesus/Yahshua saith unto him, Thomas, because thou hast seen me, thou hast believed: blessed are they that have not seen, and yet have believed.

Notice what happens when Christ says to them, "Receive ye, the Holy Ghost" and He breathed on them. The words *Holy Ghost* come from the Greek and Hebrew, which actually mean sacred (physical, pure, blameless or religious, ceremony consecrated): most holy, holy one, holy thing, saint. The word *ghost* comes from the Greek word *pneuma,* from Greek 4154 (pneo); a current of air, i.e. breath (blast) or a breeze; by analogy or figurative a spirit, i.e. (human) the rational soul, (by implication) vital principle, mental disposition, etc., or (superhuman) an angel. (Strongs Concordance #4154) **In actuality, what Christ breathed upon the disciples was a sacred mental disposition: a consecrated, vital principle—the mind of Holy Spirit.**

The mind of Holy Spirit is in complete agreement with the will of God. You must renounce your will, your ways, your ideals, your hopes, your desires, and embrace God's perfect will. Romans 12:2 (AMP) Do not be conformed to this world (this age), [fashioned after and adapted to its external, superficial customs], but be transformed (changed) by the [entire] renewal of your mind [by its new ideals and its new attitude], so that you may prove [for yourselves] what is the good and acceptable and perfect will of God, *even* the thing which is good and acceptable and perfect [in His sight for you]. When you move past the superficial customs of this world, you move into the perfect will of God.

James 5:16 (KJV) Confess your faults one to another and pray one for another, that ye may be healed. The effectual fervent prayer of a righteous man availeth much. This chapter is not about getting you to renounce your dreams and letting go of all you hope for and is certainly not the premise for this book. I have written this book because the formula hidden within this perfect prayer has unlocked so many doors for me, and all the things I have seemingly released have come to pass. Before you can truly renounce your will and embrace God's will, you must allow yourself to pardon and forgive others. If you are bound up by unforgiveness, you cannot fully embrace God's will.

There must be pardon and forgiveness before there can be renunciation. You cannot renounce something without replacing it with something else. You must replace your *will* with His *will*. Jesus/Yahshua was sharing a parable of a certain individual who had an unclean spirit, after a while, the spirits came back and found the house swept clean and put in order. Then it goes and takes seven other spirits more wicked than itself and they move in and the condition of the individual is worse than when the spirit left. (Luke11: 24-26) You must replace bad habits with good habits. Replace old thoughts with new thoughts.

Many think that the moment of triumph for Christ was on the cross, but the real triumph was in the Garden of Gethsemane when he wanted to give up, but instead he reconsidered what he had asked of the Father and said, "…nevertheless, not my will, but thy will be done." Your moment of triumph comes the second you decide to go with God's will.

James writes that some people pray amiss because they ask with the wrong motives. May I humbly submit that the whole 'crucible-of-combat' moment Christ faced in the Garden of Gethsemane had to do with the struggle within His own heart? He had to pray until he reached the place where he could say, "Nevertheless, regardless of my wants, my wishes, my desires, my needs, and my feelings, I will do what the Father has asked of me." His motive had to get to the place of total agreement with the Father's will. This is what I call praying through. Most people want to pray a quick prayer and hope that everything will work out as they desire. Nevertheless, prayer does not have to be hours long to be effective. You can pray a quick prayer, but sometimes your heart is not in the right place, and the time spent in prayer is for the alignment of *your* heart. God is not hard of hearing. He hears us when we first ask, but *our* hearts are not always in alignment with His will, so we must pray until we give in to His will.

Motive plays a bigger role in your prayer than even the words you speak because the Father already knows what we need even before we pray. Motive is the intent of what you pray. Motive is why you pray for what you pray. You need the breath of Holy Spirit like Jesus/Yahshua breathed upon the disciples, but you must be in right standing to house this presence. You must renounce your will and take up His will. That is what the LORD'S Prayer is really about—aligning one's will with the will of the Father.

Wisdom Principle: The Marriage Of Wisdom And Knowledge Gives Birth To The Perfect Will of God.

It is only when your knowledge aligns itself with the wisdom of God that the divine is born, and your thoughts begin to concede to His thoughts. His ways are higher than yours. His desires are always better than yours. His power is greater than yours. His will is better than yours. His plan is smarter than your goals. His paths are brighter than yours. His glory is greater than yours. His will is supreme!

When Moses stood before the presence of the LORD/YAHVEH, he followed the instruction to remove his shoes because he was standing on holy ground. When we need a miracle, God will always give us an instruction to carry out. Sometimes it is an illogical one, but it will always produce His perfect will. Moses obeyed the simple instruction of removing his shoes, and God in turn, performed miracle after miracle before Moses' eyes in the midst of Pharaoh and his entire kingdom.

Will you try an illogical thing, something you've never done? Will you pray with me in agreement? Repeat after me and make this declaration of your will and faith, consecrating your will unto the will of the Father. Remember Christ did not do his own will, but the will of his heavenly Father.

In the holy name of YAHVEH ELOHIM, I surrender my will

100

Unto the Great Creator and
I renounce all my human aspirations.
I align myself with the
Perfect will of the Father.
I place my destiny and my life in Your Divine hands,
In complete trust and reverence, I renounce my will.
Knowing that you will lead me in the perfect path.
I am confident that my entire human needs
Will be met and I will have peace, joy, love
And prosperity in all my days.
According to your Word, I have
Been given everything that pertains to life and Godliness.
Be it unto me according to your Word. Amen

Chapter Nine
Alignment

When something in your body is out of alignment, your body cannot function at optimal performance. Most of us have probably made a visit to a chiropractor for an adjustment; and if not, you have probably had some form of adjustment in the form of cracking your knuckles, your neck and/or your back. The alignment of our bodies is crucial to good health. If one area is off, it can become caustic to other parts of the body. When we align ourselves with God's will, we move into a dimension of power that cultivates an atmosphere for the miraculous.

You are in the middle of a spiritual awakening. Holy Spirit has been looking for someone to sync with God's perfect will. I do not believe you can manipulate God to do anything through your prayer or your great faith if it is not in His perfect will. You cannot beg God to do anything for you. The only kind of prayer He will answer is the one birthed out of brokenness and desperation fully aligned with His perfect will for your life.

Do you truly believe that God is sovereign and above all

other gods: above sickness and disease, above your stack of bills, above your crazy marriage, above the systems and the political maneuverings of this world? You don't have to be a rocket scientist or a prophet to figure out that we are living in perilous times. It is crucial to know what Holy Spirit is saying at this hour, but you must be fully aligned with God's will to hear the Word of the hour.

All the things we are seeing around the world are a domino effect of Holy Spirit being poured out upon all flesh. Holy Spirit is not just in the church; it is a global effect. Things are beginning to shake because there are those who are in alignment with the Holy Spirit and are crying out "Come Holy Spirit, come! You are welcome in this place! You have full and divine authority; do, as you will. Fill us; baptize us with your presence, with your fire, with your glory."

God is moving in mightier ways than ever before. God is so great and mighty, so vast that it is recorded in the sixth chapter of Hebrews that the men of faith opted *not* to receive the blessings of God because they said, "We're looking for a city whose architect is God." They opted out of receiving the blessings! They chose something bigger! They forfeited earthly blessings for something greater than what we can have here on earth! Can you imagine something greater than the wonderful, miraculous blessings you have received from the LORD so far? James 1:17 says every good gift is from above. Everything that is good, God gave you. There is no good outside of God.

God's Word says, "My Spirit shall fall upon all flesh..." it does not say my Spirit shall fall upon all Christians or a particular sect of people. God's Spirit is falling upon all flesh. There are changes happening in the atmosphere caused by Holy Spirit that are creating quite a stir in the hearts of men.

The flesh of man, his ego, becomes upset when we refer to God in terms of power, glory or energy: something other than a person. That is why God is choosing to fall upon all flesh. You cannot argue flesh. We can all agree everyone has flesh, which represents the ego. The work being carried out by Holy Spirit is happening supernaturally in direct relation to how the Spirit is falling upon all flesh. Do you get that? Sometimes, God allows the flesh to endure different levels of pressure to bring about a spiritual awakening.

The sooner your ego recognizes there is only one will and your flesh aligns itself with God's will, you can begin to see the miraculous. Alignment has everything to do with recognizing that we are nothing aside from Him. He is a force to be reckoned with. He is our Mighty Fortress, our Shield and Buckler, our Redeemer, our Deliverer, our Healer. In Him, we live and move and have our existence. The sovereign will of God moves us to say, "Your kingdom is come, your will is done..." God is not asking for our vote! That is why I believe that prayer is all about alignment and not so much request. God's kingdom is not a democracy; it is a theocracy with one King. His Word rules, and His Word reigns. When God declares something, there is no devil in hell, no man or woman, no entity, no power, no government that can stand up to the power of His sovereignty. When He gets ready to move, there is something in the release of His power that is incomprehensible; it does not matter if you or I understand it.

Moses heard the voice of the LORD speaking through a burning bush. When he spoke to Moses, He was very specific about His instructions on every command He gave. The children of Israel were given specific details regarding their great Exodus from Egypt. Their freedom and the success of their escape were contingent upon their alignment with the details of the instructions from the great I AM.

I value the fact that there are many who can hear the voice of the LORD. It is important to know, without a doubt, you know the voice of your God. There is always a separation between the soul and the flesh, the natural and the supernatural, but for the first time in my life I am experiencing a phenomenon where there is no divergence between my thoughts and His thoughts. That is not sacrilegious; it is simply that my thoughts are aligning with His thoughts and His ways. When you are aligned with the perfect will of God, you operate in a synchronized realm and dimension of Holy Spirit. God's will does not ask for permission; it just finds an open door, and like light, floods through it! When you turn on a light, it takes immediate dominion over darkness.

The Israelites were familiar with the sovereignty of YAHVEH. They believed whatever God said He did! They believed that YAHVEH was going to deliver them, and He did! They believed YAHVEH would feed them, and He did! They believed He would provide water in the desert, and He did! The key to answered prayer is to be so tuned to the will of the sovereign God, that whatever He has planned for you will be the final and only answer you could ever want or need.

WISDOM PRINCIPLE: THE ALIGNMENT OF YOUR MIND, WILL, AND EMOTIONS WITH GOD'S WILL EQUALS VICTORY IN EVERY AREA OF YOUR LIFE.

Chapter Ten
The Timing of Prayer

Sound the ram's horn at the New Moon, and when the moon is full, on the day of our festival; this is a decree for Israel, *an ordinance of the God of Jacob.* When God went out against Egypt, he established it as a statute for Joseph. I heard an unknown voice say: "I removed the burden from their shoulders; their hands were set free from the basket. In your distress you called and I rescued you, I answered you out of a thundercloud; I tested you at the waters of Meribah. Hear me, my people, and I will warn you—if you would only listen to me, Israel! You shall have no foreign god among you; you shall not worship any god other than me. I am the LORD your God, who brought you up out of Egypt. Open wide your mouth and I will fill it. "But my people would not listen to me; Israel would not submit to me. So I gave them over to their stubborn hearts to follow their own devices. "If my people would only listen to me, if Israel would only follow my ways how quickly I would subdue their enemies and turn my hand against their foes! Those who hate the Lord would cringe before him, and their punishment would last forever. But you would be fed with the finest of wheat; with honey from the rock I would satisfy you." Psalm 81:3-16 (NIV)

...this is a decree for Israel, *an ordinance of the God of Jacob.* The Almighty has established an ordinance and the adherence to that ordinance unlocks the power for God to subdue our enemies and turn His hand against our foes! I believe we are in the middle of a spiritual awakening. The Spirit of God is searching for those who will synchronize with His perfect will. I do not believe we can manipulate God to do anything through prayer or even through faith. You cannot beg Him enough, cry enough or confess-to-possess enough to make it happen. The only kind of prayer He answers is the kind birthed out of His own will. You're probably thinking I am not familiar with the great faith teachers that taught us to use our faith to get whatever we decree, like Hannah, who cried so much until God gave her a baby.

Do you believe that God is sovereign above all other gods, above sickness, above disease, above your stack of bills, above your unhappy marriage, above the systems and the political maneuverings of this world? I think we can all agree we live in perilous times. If we truly believe that God is sovereign and His Word is true, then we must agree He has a perfect plan for each of our lives regardless of how crazy times may be. I have already iterated and reiterated that God's will *is* done. If His will is done, where does our faith and our will play into the answers we desire when we pray? I am by no means saying that I don't believe in faith. I am a man of great faith. I stand in agreement with the sick, the afflicted and those in desperation and believe for the miracle even when everyone else has given up. I'm the preacher who doesn't give up even when the close of kin have pulled the plug and the doctors leave the room. I stand in faith despite the stifling, oppressive spirit of hopelessness that often fills the ICU or CCU room. I am the one who walks into the hospital room when doctors have given absolutely no hope, and I decree and declare God's power, authority and His Word/His will! But it's just that, I believe in the God of miracles; I don't believe *in* miracles. There's a big difference. The difference in my prayer and someone else's prayer is *timing.* When we synchronize our spirit with God's timing and align our will with His will, we will begin to see more miracles, the many signs and wonders and even the mighty exploits that Yahshua said we would and could do. Because he ascended to the Father to make intercession for us!

You've heard the saying, "A day late and a dollar short." Some people are perpetually late. I believe timing is more important than most believers realize. What makes people be late? It's not the devil putting up obstacles. It's their flesh!

As I mentioned in the previous chapter, the ego becomes upset when we talk about God in terms of power, glory or energy—something other than a *person*. We try to figure Him out as an image that we can relate to, but the truth of the matter is, He cannot be contained in an earthly vessel made of clay. He is unfathomable. He doesn't fit any image. He declared himself as the "I AM THAT I AM" to Moses because He cannot confine Himself to any earthly explanation or definition. Can you begin to understand and comprehend His sovereignty? He is establishing His power and authority, and when we align ourselves with that, His will comes into full view. His Word rules and His Word reigns! God's will or His thoughts do not have to wait for permission by our prayer to be carried out or to come to fruition. They just simply move with freedom in my mind because I'm already in agreement with His will and not my will.

God is waiting to hear you crying out, to see you broken before Him. The Psalmist wrote, "LORD, who shall abide in thy tabernacle? Who shall dwell in thy holy hill? The meek and the lowly shall enter in. Only the pure in heart shall enter in." (Psalm 15) A broken and contrite heart does so much for God's heart. There are a lot of people who know God's will for them is to prosper and be in health; however, they are moving in their own timing. Until you quit trying to control your own destiny, you will not be able to align yourself with His perfect will. He is gracious, kind and merciful and will allow good things to happen even when we are pushing our way through life. But it is not until we are in full alignment with His perfect will that we can see the fullness of our purpose. When you move into the place of His perfect will, you move into a place where you do not have enough words or even know what to pray; your prayers become insufficient.

If you are living your life with *your* desire above His, what can be your destiny? It's a gamble! However, when His desires become your desires you lock into your purpose and destiny for your life.

WISDOM PRINCIPLE: GOD IS NOT LOOKING FOR PERFECTION; HE IS LOOKING FOR PRECISION.

God is never late; He is always on time. Amen? He is a God of precision. So you must align yourself to His precise timing. You must align your mind, your body, your spirit, your attitude, your thoughts, your words, your actions with the timing of the perfect will of the Father. That means, *"...nevertheless, not my will, but thy will be done."*

In Psalm 81, the writer calls for the sounding of a trumpet, which of course means that something is about to happen. There is a particular time when the trumpet is to be sounded. "...when the moon is new." I don't know too many who are consciously aware of the lunar cycles, but they are part of God's perfect timing. Most people I know pretty much ignore the moon. They complain when the sun hides behind clouds or gets forced out by storms. Perhaps when the subject of the moon comes up, you think of werewolves and the like because many of us are accustomed to the association between full moons and haunted, scary stories we've heard growing up. However, long before the vampires and werewolves, God was using the lunar cycles to teach His people when to align themselves for their battles and victories. It is interesting that the modern world operates on a solar calendar, and God's people follow a lunar calendar. The thing about God's timing is, if you do not move according to His timing someone else will. God led His people, who listened to His messengers, through the wilderness with lunar cycles, pillars of fire, clouds of smoke and stars. Wow! What a wonderful display of God's majesty, and here we are praying for "things" God already knows we need. We beg for miracles when every morning and every evening, He paints a beautiful sky, and His canvas fills with the colors of the rainbow as the sun goes down. God still uses these elements and speaks to those who have ears to hear.

When you ask God for something, when do you want Him to answer or move on fulfill your need? We want what we want when we want it. We want everything in *our* timing; and yet, how much time, how many minutes or hours of the 24 He gives do we devote to Him? I don't know and have never met a believer who doesn't want God to promote them, bless them, heal them, provide for them, increase their finances, etc., etc. But how few are willing to invest much time reading a book that teaches how to pray effectively and in alignment with God's perfect will and timing.

You may never experience or understand the full blessings of biblical economics unless you understand the importance of God's timing. Many Christians are more cognitive and aware of the meaning of Friday the 13th than they are of the seasons and festivals God appointed in the Scriptures.

Have you ever been late to work? If your job depends on it, you can find a way to be on time especially if it affects your money. God wants to declare Himself mighty to you, but how much time are you devoting to Him? People have time to read-up on all the latest Hollywood gossip, Oprah, the latest fashion trends, but they have no time for God's house when the weekend rolls around. Wal-Mart probably gets more visits from Christians than God's house. People will get up in the middle of the night to shop at their nearest Wal-Mart just to get the best price, but how many would go to such extremes to be in God's presence? Many say, "Oh, Pastor, God is with me even when I'm laying down in my bed." They that wait upon the LORD… People can stand in line patiently waiting reading a People magazine, but what happens to their attitudes when the service at their local church goes a little longer than usual? I live down the road from a mega church, where policemen are needed to control the traffic flow. Many of my friends and neighbors crowd into a "Starbucks" atmosphere building and often watch a large screen of the pastor's message when he is unavailable or indisposed, but there are no complains because the fellowship is good, and they get in and out in an hour! How can you come into alignment with the perfect will of God when you are operating under your own will, and you have more time for Wal-Mart than you do for His house? Okay, sorry for the tirade; it's over.

Okay, maybe, just one more example: Recently, Wal-Mart implemented a policy change concerning their employees. The policy stated employees would be docked for every minute they were late. It was determined that Wal-Mart saved over 28 million dollars in one district alone simply by docking the employee's pay for being late. The employees of course sued and won the lawsuit. What is wrong with this picture? What kind of message is being conveyed? God has a specific timing for everything He does. If you don't show up on time, you will miss it! It's that simple. Either you are on God's timeline, or you're on your ego's timeline. And we've already established that our egos can get us in the worst mess if we listen to it.

I believe this is where many prayers go unanswered, because so many believers are just a minute or two late. "But Pastor, what about God's mercy and grace?" His mercy and grace are evident in that we are all still here! God has established everything with precision and within that precision is a timeframe that *must* be adhered. …this is a decree for Israel, *an ordinance of the God of Jacob!*

The fact that we are given such power through faith to speak to a mountain and make it move means nothing if we are not in God's timing. "Mustard seed faith" is an amazing and powerful concept, but pointless in the wrong dimension. How many people do you know that have stood in front of Pikes Peak and made it move into the ocean? Wrong dimension! But when speaking of the mountain of problems we are often faced with, it makes perfect sense. And yet, timing is still the key factor. If I am praying for a mountain of debt to move in my life, but I'm late to work every day, the faith to move that mountain is pointless! What makes Christians think that through prayer one can violate the perfectly aligned ecological system of God and not incur the wrath of disturbing it? Impossible! There is a reaction to everything that falls out of sequence. Do you think that God is going to allow something to come out of perfect alignment because He feels sorry for one person? His mercy endureth to all generations! Yes! But His *will* is and has always been done! Herein lies the mystery of faith. We can have what we want if we doubt not. If we align ourselves with precision to the perfect will of God, we will then want what He wants when He wants. "Pastor, what about Psalm 37:4 where God says He will give you the desires of your heart?" Exactly! He will give your heart what it should desire.

Acts 2:20 (KJV) The sun shall be turned into darkness, and the moon into blood, before that great and notable day of the LORD come. Have you ever wondered why the Bible says the moon will turn to blood? Remember, we are still talking about the moon and the lunar calendar. What is contained in the blood of Yahshua? According to Scripture, the genetic bloodline was significantly important for the coming Messiah. Life and DNA are contained in the blood. A blood moon is a sign of something significant taking place in the heavenlies. God puts up gigantic billboards in the heavens so that no one can miss it. His announcements are never small.

Most everyone I know enjoys sunny days, probably because of the instant benefit. The chemical response of our bodies to the sun is the release of serotonin. Serotonin is the chemical our brains produce that causes us to experience feelings of happiness. So, my inquisitive nature and my desire to research a matter causes me to query, what role the moon plays in our lives. I must say I have never met a moon gazer; however, I have always had a fascination with the *ball of cheese* that hangs out with the stars at night. The first thing that comes to mind, as far as the role the moon plays within our galaxy, is its role in the alignment of our galaxy. The moon causes the ocean tides to rise and fall; it can cause the internal parts of the earth to groan. When the earth begins to tremble and quake and tsunamis erupt, it is due to the moon's gravitational pull. Silent as it is, unnoticed by most, the moon is obedient to the commands of the great Creator. It shows up faithfully every evening carrying out the perfect will of the Almighty. The Perfect Prayer has a similar pull on our spirits and our physical bodies. It aligns us mentally, spiritually and physically to the predestined will of our Father.

I had to do a little studying to fully understand the difference between a new moon and a full moon: apogee and perigee. Apogee and perigee refer to the distance from the Earth to the moon. *Apogee* is the farthest point from Earth. *Perigee* is the closest point to Earth, and it is in this stage the moon appears larger. Looking at the moon in the sky without anything to compare it to, you wouldn't notice any size difference. But the difference in size can in fact be quite significant. Jewish tradition calls for a celebration of the new moon where one chants the Hallal accompanied by the blasts of the shofar. Although prayer began as a simple cry to the Almighty, Christ came along and taught the disciples how to pray. Did you catch that? He *taught* them to pray. There is a protocol to prayer that few understand or recognize.

Malachi 2:7 (NIV) For the lips of a priest ought to preserve knowledge, because he is the messenger of the Lord Almighty and people seek instruction from his mouth. God uses His chain of command established long before the first prayer was uttered.

Prayer is all about alignment. If a car is out of alignment, it could ruin a new set of tires very quickly. An alignment costs much less than a new set of tires or a new car. Similarly, the same principle applies to the kingdom. If something is out of alignment in your life, it is much easier to align yourself with God's perfect will than trying to do things your way. I'm not implying that you may be deep in sin and are completely separated from God; instead it just means you may be out of line, out of order just a bit. Better to receive a minor adjustment than a correction. You could easily end up in the ditch if you are not properly aligned. When you begin asking why things are not working out for you, perhaps, you should go back to the last instruction you received from God, whether through Scripture or through your man of God. And may I interject, every believer must have a man of God and belong to a local body of believers.

WISDOM PRINCIPLE: GOD WILL NEVER PROMOTE YOU PAST YOUR LAST ACT OF DISOBEDIENCE.

The word *alignment* has burned in my spirit for years, perhaps, because I am a perfectionist, and I am obsessed with making sure things are perfectly aligned and in order. By the same token, I realize we can never attain perfection. And living for God is not about perfection, but rather about aligning ourselves to His predestined plans and purpose.

Psalm 138:2 (AMP) I will worship toward Your holy temple and praise Your name for Your loving-kindness and for Your truth *and* faithfulness; for You have exalted above all else Your name and Your word *and* You have magnified Your word above all Your name! The writer is facing a particular direction when paying homage to God. This may seem insignificant to some, but the person who is in search of unlocking God's power for a miracle will do whatever it takes. Every time someone in the Bible experienced a supernatural miracle, there was always a specific set of details and instructions they were required to follow. Sometimes, the changes were life altering. The day of small, minor changes is over! God is looking for radical change in the body of Christ.

God is not under the jurisdiction of the laws of earth or our definition of success and prosperity. Would you agree the realm of

Holy Spirit, the atmosphere where God lives and abides, is different than anything we can understand with our natural minds? God dwells in a totally different realm and order of sequence than we do. So, if we are going to tap into the power of God, does it not merit that we must move into His realm?

I have a powerful revelation and understanding of: Isaiah 59:19 (KJV) So shall they fear the name of the Lord from the west, and his glory from the rising of the sun. When the enemy shall come in like a flood, the Spirit of the Lord shall lift up a standard against him.

When the enemy comes in like a flood, God raises the standard, and we are called to rise to the level of that new standard. You avoid confrontation with your enemy by coming up to God's level. Your best weapon against the enemy is raising your standard. Raise your standard of worship! Raise your standard of how you treat your spouse! Raise your standard regarding your commitment to your church! Raise your standard of how you serve and bless your man or woman of God! Raise your standard of your productivity at work or at school! Lift up the standard and sound the alarm!

God did not forget about you when the enemy came in like a flood. The first thing many believers do is blame God when they are enduring difficulty in their lives. A few years ago an unbelievable devastation took place in Indonesia when a record-breaking tsunami destroyed thousands of lives and decimated the shoreline. The people who were affected by the tsunami were those who stood there gazing as the waves began to swell, and the tide began to rise to incredible levels. It was reported that very few animals perished in the wake of the disaster. The animals climbed to higher ground because they are finely tuned in to the earth's pulse—the frequencies of the earth.

Are you tuned in to the frequencies and the pulse of His Presence? I believe God is calling for us to do things that veer from the normal and the ordinary. He is calling for us to do things that do nothing for Him, but instead create changes in our minds, our bodies and our souls. It is vitally important that you understand this principle in order to unlock all that is in this model prayer. You must align yourself with God's Word.

Romans 12:2 (NIV) Do not conform to the pattern of this world, but be transformed by the renewing of your mind. Then you will be able to test and approve what God's will is, His good, pleasing and perfect will. I wonder how many of God's people are unwittingly content to be in the good will of God instead of His perfect will? The good, acceptable, and perfect will of God are not a plethora of choices; it should be a progression! When you begin your walk with the LORD, you are in His *good* will. After a while, you move into His *acceptable* will because now, you are beginning to adjust to your new lifestyle. Some days you're up and some days you're down relying on His mercy to sustain you in the acceptable level. But before too long, you progress to the *perfect* will of God, which is where this prayer positions and postures you!

God wants to promote you, to bless you, and has wonderful things in store for you, but you must get into His perfect will to unlock these things. You cannot say you have aligned yourself with God's perfect will while you are double-minded and wishy-washy about whether you should go to church, whether you should tithe, whether you should be faithful… Many believers are simply living in the acceptable and good will of God, never tapping into that perfect will! You can live in the good will of God and still make it to heaven, but if you're looking for the "life more abundantly" that Jesus/Yahshua promised, you will have to step up to the perfect will of God. Lift up the standard!

God will use people to connect you to His perfect will. When God wants to bless you, He puts a right person in your life. When evil wants to distract you, a wrong person enters your life. God's perfect will is discovered when you remain in agreement with those *divine* connections. So often, people will say, "I don't understand why God hasn't answered my prayer," when all the while, they have disconnected from the golden connection God sent their way to bring about the miracle. You may be disconnecting from a God-connection, a divine connection that God sent to heal you or help you through your tough times because you were looking for someone who looked just like you. Sometimes, God will carry out His will with the most unlikely people in your life. In the dimension of His presence and power, you do not have a choice because His will *is* done. Ultimately, God's will is already done here on Earth as it is already in Heaven because of the difference in time and space. From God's perspective His will is already done! You just have not entered the dimension or the galaxy where it is already done. I

115

believe The Perfect Prayer, as recited by Christ in Matthew 11, holds the keys to the kingdom of God.

Matthew 16:19 (KJV) And I will give unto thee the keys of the kingdom of heaven: and whatsoever thou shalt bind on earth shall be bound in heaven: and whatsoever thou shalt loose on earth shall be loosed in heaven. Notice how this ties in with The Perfect Prayer. "Our heavenly Father, hallowed is your name. Your kingdom is come, your will is done *as in heaven so also earth...*" We can only bind on earth what is already bound in heaven. This may sound like God is an absolute God, and He is! He is absolutely always right, and His will is already done. That is destiny!

You may not be able to perceive any "destiny" in what you're going through right now. In the Old Testament, God instructed Abraham to walk before Him blameless. That does not mean he had to be perfect, just obedient! I am aware that many preachers, teachers and evangelists are teaching that you can have your best life now, but you must understand that your best life is connected to your obedience. Moses, the most powerful figure in ancient Judaism, never got to experience the "Promised Land" because he fell short. Moses was the lawgiver, and yet, he violated one of God's laws, and it cost him the promise.

Hebrews 11:10 (AMP) For he was [waiting expectantly and confidently] looking forward to the city which has fixed *and* firm foundations, whose Architect *and* Builder is God. God's will is a place, a residence! If you want to go to the place of His presence, you must be in right order with God's Word. You must be a holder of the keys to the Kingdom to enter. God cannot allow anything but His will into this place, this residence, because this would make Him subject to someone else's will! This is why it is so important that your prayer be fashioned as Jesus/Yahshua instructed the disciples.

God wants you to have blessings daily! In The Perfect Prayer, we ask God to give us the bread of our "daily" needs and leave us serene. When God blesses you, the outcome is always serenity. You must understand something about prayer. Prayer is not a declaration or request to make God do something for you. Prayer is an alignment with the Word of God. It transforms you into the pattern of His perfect will.

CHAPTER ELEVEN
THE PURPOSE OF PRAYER

The first of the Ten Commandments is actually an establishment of the relationship God wants to have with His people and how to relate to Him. "I AM the LORD, your God. Thou shalt have no other gods before me and have no graven images..." When you establish God as God in your life, it is easy to then follow the other nine commandments.

Most people believe the first commandment is, "Thou shalt love the LORD your God with all your heart, mind, and body..." Moreover, I find it interesting that nowhere in any of the Ten Commandments does God command us to love Him. He wants us to love Him of our own choosing. Yahshua said, "If you love me, keep my commandments." God wants us to worship Him, and the only real way we can desire to worship Him is to understand and know His name and the prayer central to His heart. A quick review of the Ten Commandments reveals that the first three commandments are focused on God, then the Sabbath, then He calls for honor to those in authority over us, finally he lays out a perfect formula to insure we get along with each other.

The Ten Commandments

1. You shall have no other gods before Me.
2. You shall not make idols.
3. You shall not take the name of the LORD your God in vain.
4. Remember the Sabbath day, to keep it holy.
5. Honor your father and your mother.
6. You shall not murder.
7. You shall not commit adultery.
8. You shall not steal.
9. You shall not bear false witness against your neighbor.
10. You shall not covet.

In the New Testament, Christ launches his ministry and teaches people how to pray in order to unlock the secret of the universe, which is worship. That is what is so significant about The Perfect Prayer. It is a precursor for what will happen when you align yourself to God's will. It is important to understand this prayer is neither a plea nor a petition. You do not have to beg God for anything; you just have to know how to align yourself for the answer. Remember, it was Jesus/Yahshua who sought to teach his disciples how to pray with this powerful combination of words, beginning with giving honor to the Father. Christ never directed anyone to pray to him; he said pray in this manner: "Our heavenly Father..." He puts himself in the middle of your mess, your hardships become his hardships; he's in the middle of what you are facing right now and he says, "Let's pray, *Our heavenly Father, holy is your name...*"

The Paternoster or The Our Father is the best-known agreeable factor among believers of every tradition. You can access every human need through this model prayer. Did you receive that within your spirit? You can access *every* human need through this prayer! I believe The LORD'S Prayer positions us physically, emotionally, spiritually and mentally for the manifestation of the impossible. Many of us have been brought up to believe that prayer is a way to coerce God or move Him to do what we request. The only thing that moves God is His Word. Prayer puts us in the right position and in the right frame of mind to enter the portal of the dimensions of His power.

The beautiful book, <u>The Prayer of Jabez</u>, inspired from the Old Testament prayer offered by Jabez, which I mentioned earlier in chapter one, was an overnight success because it promised the reader success and increase. I have met people who believed very strongly in this little book, but did not believe in the principles of tithes and offerings or sowing financial seeds, and yet, they believed that reciting the "magic" words offered by Jabez would grant them their increase. There is nothing wrong with believing God for increase and success, if you are in right order with His standards concerning the laws of sowing and reaping. If one of my two beautiful children made a request of me, and all the while I knew they had been stealing from me and dishonoring me, I would hesitate to bless them and would not continue to enable their wrongful behavior. What makes us think we can ask God for blessings and increase without changing our behavior?

In the New Testament book of Matthew, you can read The LORD'S Prayer, which most us have grown up hearing and reciting. In the King James version of Scripture and other similar translations, the prayer speaks futuristically about the Father, His kingdom and His will. The Aramaic version of the prayer declares those things as being available *now*, and the ending of the prayer transcends time. "Hallowed *is* your name, Your kingdom *is* come, Your will *is* done…" The Perfect Prayer is an alignment of your past, present and future. I heard someone say, and I have often used this adage over the years: "God never consults your past to determine your future." It sounds good in theory, but the truth is, God looks at us from the perspective of a continuum. When we obey His precepts, laws, and ordinances and regard them sweeter than honey as the Psalmist wrote, He schedules a promotion or some form of increase! Then God will use our past, our present and our future to establish the standard of blessings for our lives. Notice what David wrote in the Psalm I quoted above, "The statutes of the LORD are perfect…sweeter also than honey and the honeycomb." When you love God's statues and His laws, it is proof you have mastered your will to conform to His will. Your attitude has changed; your focus has changed; the intent of your heart has come into alignment with His heart. Ah, sweet surrender and sweet agreement.

In the supernatural, there is no time. No tick tock... It is a continuum from one dimension to another. We are eternal beings. What happens here on earth doesn't really count in the scope of timelessness; it is simply a passageway into His presence. Whatever you need, wish or desire is in the "now" part of your faith, and everything our spirit man aspires is in the glory of His ageless timelessness.

Jesus/Yahshua wanted the disciples to know how to pray effectively. They had grown dependent on his power and anointing. He wanted them to realize where his power came from and how to put their trust in their heavenly Father. He wanted them to understand he had come to the Earth to do his Father's will, not his own. He often said he only did and said what his Father wanted. 1 John 3:8b (AMP) The Son of God appeared for this purpose, to destroy the works of the devil. If Christ truly destroyed the works of the devil, why are so many Christians always talking about the devil and his power? Yahshua defeated the devil once and for all! Jesus' model prayer says nothing about coming against the devils; it simply says "...and separate us from the evil one." What does separate mean to you? Does it mean you talk about him everyday? Does it mean you give him credit when bad things happen in your life? No! It means you separate yourself from him and all he stands for! The definition of the word *separation* according to Miriam Webster's Dictionary is: the act or process of separating: the state of being separated: 2 a: a point, line, or means of division b: an intervening space, termination of a contractual relationship.

The first thing the disciples had to understand was the fact that God's will is *already* done, no demons to fight, no devils to conquer – just acknowledge "Your will is done..." We have been taught, through the prosperity and the blessed life messages, that you simply zero in on what you "want", focus on the "want" and stay on it until your petition is fulfilled. Prayer is not for the purpose of carrying out *our* will. This type of petitioning is no different than the "law of attraction" taught by many secularists. And while you will attract what you focus on, only that which is born of the Spirit overcomes the world. In reality, we do not have one thing that God

120

has not given us. The Bible says, "Whatever is born of the Spirit overcomes the world." Many people acquire things and make decisions by their own power and strength. They are producing miss-creations that are born outside of the Spirit.

WISDOM PRINCIPLE: THE PROBLEM WITH ACQUIRING THINGS OUTSIDE OF THE SPIRIT IS YOU WILL HAVE TO REMAIN OUTSIDE OF THE SPIRIT TO KEEP THEM.

Jesus/Yahshua established this prayer as the model for structuring our prayer. What else could *"Pray in this manner..."* mean? He meant for us to model our prayers after The LORD'S Prayer. The model prayer, when examined through the eyes of our Savior, holds a totally different concept than what we have been taught.

"As in heaven, so also on earth," is pivotal to the way we pray. Many of us try to make something happen in heaven based on what we want here on earth. The Aramaic translation shows the proper order of how things work. "As in heaven" comes first, then, "on earth" follows. You may have heard these two dimensions referred to as parallel universes.

Matthew 18:18 (AMP) I assure you *and* most solemnly say to you, whatever you bind [forbid, declare to be improper and unlawful] on earth shall have [already] been bound in heaven, and whatever you loose [permit, declare lawful] on earth shall have [already] been loosed in heaven. That means we can bind or loose whatever is already bound or loosed in heaven.

WISDOM PRINCIPLE: FAITH PRODUCES WHAT I WANT; TRUST PRODUCES WHAT GOD WANTS.

The Perfect Prayer is about absolute faith and trust in God. It is a prayer of alignment, of faith, of direction, of financial provision, of repentance and also a ritual prayer. Ritual means practice. We have to rehearse or practice God's will. The Perfect Prayer is perfect because it covers all the basics pertaining to our physical and spiritual life.

2 Peter 1:3 (AMP) For His divine power has bestowed on us

121

[absolutely] everything necessary for [a dynamic spiritual] life and godliness, through true *and* personal knowledge of Him who called us by His own glory and excellence. I love the Amplified Version because it uses the word "absolutely" meaning without a doubt, in an absolute manner or condition.

In every believer's life, there comes a time when you must trust God explicitly. Even after you have prayed and stood in faith, you are not always going to know the answer to your prayer. There is a quote posted in one of the Sunday School classrooms at our church that says, "Prayers that are not prayed will never be answered." We must understand prayer deals with the human psyche. Anything you focus on or repetitively dwell on autonomously begins to propel you toward actions that lead to the fruition of that to which you are focused. That is why some books that teach the principles of success have made millions. As you learn to focus on the things you want, your mind begins to cause you to do whatever it takes to achieve success.

Does focusing on success place you in the center of God's perfect will? Probably not. What good is it to have attained a certain level of wealth if you are still unhappy at the end of the day? God wants to bring us to a place where we trust Him, not only for our future needs, but also more importantly for our immediate needs. "Give us the bread of our daily needs..."

Many people pray out of desperation, and as I mentioned in a previous chapter, God can use desperation as He did in the case of Hannah's desire for a baby. But God wants us to come to a place where we trust Him and are willing to wait in serenity for the answer. We all want the turbulence to stop; we want a little serenity in the midst of our chaotic lives. God wants to bring you to the place where you are serene and not stressed over the outcome of each day no matter what it brings. As believers, we can have the calm assurance that "This is the day the LORD has made; I will rejoice and be glad in it." The Bible says, "In everything give thanks for this is the will of God." It's pretty difficult to give thanks if you are not walking in serenity. The will of God is just that, the *will* of God.

Many are praying for that perfect man or perfect woman to come into their lives. The only perfect gifts are from above, from the Father of lights according to James 1:17. When God gives you something, He is not going to add sorrow to it. If the love of your life leaves you high and dry, that is proof that it was not from above because when God blesses you, He puts a right person in your life.

The Word says God delights in the prosperity of His saints. The problem is most people want to delight in the prosperity, but not always in the One who made the provision possible. God wants to be our delight. He wants us to trust in Him and not lean to our own understanding (our jobs, our spouses, our money, our own strength). God wants to put you on the path of blessings and abundance. To be on the right path, you must be a person of purpose, not someone who is waiting for an opportunity to walk through the open door of someone else's misfortune; that's an opportunist. God is calling for us to become people of destiny. It's not enough to know your purpose. There are many people who know their purpose but are not fulfilling their destiny because they are not actively doing what they are purposed to do on a daily basis! You cannot get in shape if you go to the gym once a month or even once a week! You must be willing to dedicate yourself to a regimen that is consistent and of course then there is discipline. Living in your destiny will force you to do the exercises that produce the greatest results.

WISDOM PRINCIPLES: DESTINY PUSHES YOUR PURPOSE INTO PRODUCING!

WISDOM PRINCIPLE: AGREEMENT WITH YOUR PURPOSE ACCELERATES THE FULFILLMENT OF YOUR DESTINY.

A person of purpose puts God first in all areas of life. What makes you think that your prayer is more eloquent than the model prayer Jesus/Yahshua prayed himself to the Father? This prayer unlocks the bread of our daily needs. Everything that pertains to life and godliness is yours when you align yourself to God's perfect will for your life!

WISDOM PRINCIPLE: SUCCESS IS GOD'S WORD OPERATING IN EVERY AREA OF YOUR LIFE.

At the pool of Bethesda, an angel of the LORD would stir up the waters once a year, and the first person to jump into the water would receive healing. It was like a "magical" moment. You cannot make it to the pool if you are not at the right place waiting for the stirring of the waters. Sometimes, desperation is the driving force for those willing to wait as long as it takes to be the first one in. That's why Isaiah wrote, "They that wait upon the LORD shall renew their strength…" Your healing may have already arrived, but you've been too preoccupied with other things, and now you're too tired or unmotivated to get up and jump in the water. Come on, get up! Commit yourself to your church, to your man of God and get ready for the next stirring, and jump in!

God has given us the actual formula through The Perfect Prayer for what He wants us to have. Perhaps, this concept is offensive to some who believe that their prayers float on a cloud right into the throne room of God. Are you beginning to see what God's *will* really is about? It is not about your needs, your wants, your desperation or even, your ability to believe you shall receive. It is all about what God wants each of us to have, what He has already planned for us to have. The Perfect Prayer aligns you to the perfect will of God that is already established in Heaven.

When the Apostle Paul instructed us to put on the whole armor of God, he was demonstrating the need for arming oneself with the necessary tools for victory. The Perfect Prayer is our armament for winning over the flesh to receive what God has for us. When you align yourself with The Perfect Prayer, it changes your perspective on your situation and circumstances. This prayer exposes a different perspective; it causes you to see the matter from the eyes of God and not your own indecisive, unstable emotions.

A few years ago when we first bought our present home, we had to pay property taxes based on the full value of the home. We paid several thousands of dollars above the valuation of the home, and later found out, we could ask for a reduction in taxes based on the need for repairs on the house because it had sat vacant for two years. When we met with the tax office, they informed us the time for negotiating had already passed by several months. I asked to speak to the person in charge and began to pray The Perfect Prayer. The next person made it clear there was no way they would issue a refund because it was a state mandated law. I was told once you have paid taxes, by Texas standards, they cannot issue a refund and that was that. I prayed the prayer again and asked if there was anyone else I could speak with. They gave me the name of the person in charge, and she reiterated what everyone before had already said. "We cannot issue a refund because it is the state law." I prayed the prayer a third time. A short time passed, and she contacted me to let me know that they would be issuing a refund for the full amount. The check was in the mail! The keys to the Kingdom have unlocked blessings that go beyond my scope of asking, thinking or understanding. Praying this prayer over and over may seem ritualistic or repetitious, but there is power in rituals ordained by God.

CHAPTER TWELVE
PATTERNS AND PRAYER

What is a ritual? A ritual describes a ceremony central to an act of worship or as a repeated act that establishes patterns of conduct. When you do something ritualistically, you become extremely and acutely familiar with it. It becomes a behavioral pattern, good, bad or otherwise.

We are all ritualistic people. We wake each morning and shower, brush our teeth and prepare for our day. Thanks to the rituals that our parents instilled in us, we have healthy teeth and clean bodies. The same applies with the rituals of our spiritual lives. Rituals are an intrinsic part of our mental, emotional, and spiritual makeup. Perhaps, it will be more palatable to your spiritual taste buds if I refer to rituals as patterns.

Once you have learned to ride a bike, even if you have not ridden in twenty years, there are patterns in your brain that help you quickly recall how to navigate on two wheels. These are indelible marks that have been stored in your brain. Do not sell yourself short; you are an incredible being created by God with a totally different genetic code than any other person. You are fearfully and wonderfully made. Your patterns are unique to you. There are patterns God wanted to establish within His people with regards to prayer. It is only natural to want to call upon the name of the LORD, although many people do not retrieve this pattern until they are faced with a difficult situation.

We create indelible patterns for our lives through repetition. Those patterns can also cause us to end up in a rut. Have you ever been stuck in an unhealthy rut? It is because you have created certain patterns that lead you to the same destructive behavior even when you do not want to go down that road. Patterns are the reason alcoholics find it difficult to *change* their behavior. The only way to break through these ritualistic patterns is to connect with the spiritual unseen where these patterns are rooted. You must replace a negative pattern with a positive one. By the same token, you must connect to the realm of the supernatural to create good patterns, established through worship.

WISDOM PRINCIPLE: CHANGE IS THE ONLY CATALYST TO THE CHARACTER OF CHRIST.

Romans 12:2 (AMP) Do not be conformed to this world (this age), [fashioned after and adapted to its external, superficial customs], but be transformed (changed) by the [entire] renewal of your mind [by its new ideals and its new attitude], so that you may prove [for yourselves] what is the good and acceptable and perfect will of God, *even* the thing which is good and acceptable and perfect [in His sight for you].

When we flow with the patterns of Holy Spirit, we align ourselves with God's will, and it establishes a connection or a bridge between God and us. He dwells in the place of His will. That is why you must align yourself with The Perfect Prayer because if there are two wills, eventually, one wins out over the other. If you have two wills, nothing can happen in the dimension of the Spirit because it's like being double-minded. Picture an attorney trying to probate the last will and testament of a deceased person who left two wills. The heirs will end up with little or nothing because each heir will want to contest the *wills* to discover the intended will of the deceased.

There is no question that God wants to bless you and prosper you, now in this lifetime, but you must stay on track for His will to be carried out, not your own. Two wills cancel out each other, and the only ones experiencing any success are the attorneys fighting it out. The book of James says, "A double-minded man is unstable in all his ways." God's perfect will is manifest when you remain in agreement with the people divinely appointed to you. In the dimension of His presence and His perfect will, you do not have a choice because His will is already done. I've never met anyone who did not want God's will for his or her life. You must be willing to have absolute faith and trust in His will.

I find myself praying this prayer at all hours of the day. I used to get up every morning to be at early Morning Prayer at our church. I did this ritualistically for years until God spoke to me about my verbose prayers and let me know that prayer is a daily, continuous conversation with the Father. A member of my church was describing a movie he watched about the 9/11 attacks on the twin towers in New York. He said that one of the men trapped in the rubble of the disaster was fading into a coma. As he was beginning to lose consciousness, he began to pray the LORD'S Prayer, and he lived to tell his story. This man religiously recited the LORD'S Prayer in the translation he grew up with, and this ritual ultimately saved his life!

When we become desperate, faith comes rising from the dark cavernous recesses of our minds, and we ultimately end up calling upon God. A simple alignment in the midst of chaos, mayhem and destruction could ultimately save your life. I always say, never give up or turn on the only one who can help you. If you can get in the place of His presence, which is connected to His perfect will, you will find He is your absolute protector and your fortress.

I believe God is leading the church into a ritual or pattern of The Perfect Prayer on a daily basis. This prayer holds the keys to the kingdom.

What happens when we pray about certain issues in the manner we have become accustomed to? Sometimes nothing. Why, because we have not tapped into the will of God. The patterns of the path to health and wealth are not visible in the natural, but are intrinsic to your spirit man. You must get out of the flesh and move into your spirit man. The Perfect Prayer allows your spirit to guide you into the realm of the unseen presence of God where the patterns are. Your flesh man may be on its way to do something, but along

128

the way he sees something that entices him, and there you go! The spirit man is neither subject to this world nor its enticements. It is subject only to the laws of the Spirit realm, hence the battle between ego and spirit.

I had to personally break the cycle of defeat over my life by displacing my father's destructive addictive patterns that eventually led to his premature death. He was a strong, virile man, unfortunately with a penchant for alcohol. I remember coming to a place in my life where God showed me how to break the patterns of defeat that had been transferred from my father and his father. I had to stop the cycle of these generational curses in order to gain my own freedom and stop the curses from perpetuating to the next generation. I had to align myself to the patterns of Holy Spirit to unlock the power of God's will for my life. You are not beholden to your father's sins or the sins of their fathers; you can be free!

The Bible tells us the effectual, fervent prayer of a righteous man availeth much. The problem with many people's prayers is not the lack of fervency, rather, a lack of efficacy. I believe many feel very fervently about their prayers, whether for themselves or for others, but it is the effectual, fervent prayer that avails much. There are many who pray for hours every day, but their prayers are mostly petitions for unmet needs. They may even be praying for someone else's needs above their own. However, the "effectual" part of their prayer is lacking because they are not in alignment with the patterns of the will of the Father.

Perhaps, The LORD'S Prayer should have been titled, The Prayer of God's Will because it really is all about God's will for your life. Are you beginning to see the patterns that prove this theory? I suppose this book could have been much shorter, with fewer chapters, but I have purposely taken the time to supply you with as much research and a strong scriptural foundation to reveal the power of *the* prayer.

How do you tap into these patterns? Obviously, one must have the right key to unlock a treasure. As a child, I always dreamed of finding a hidden treasure! I have always had a fascination for treasures and things that remain hidden. I could envision myself entering into a dark cave and stumbling onto a treasure-trove of gold! I do not just want to earn money; I want to find it, I want to win it! I want God to do something, so no one gets the glory but

Him. That is what this prayer will do for you as you create the patterns of Holy Spirit on a daily basis. Isaiah 45:3 (KJV) And I will give thee the treasures of darkness, and hidden riches of secret places, that thou mayest know that I, the Lord, which call thee by thy name, am the God of Israel.

Are you ready to receive the formula for a daily regimen of blessings? Scientific research supports that electrical currents flow through our bodies, and we are affected by the electromagnetic force of earth, sun and moon. The heart stops beating if the electrical current that makes it beat is interrupted. A defibrillator can revive someone with an electrical shock. The Perfect Prayer, in like manner, can resuscitate you with the power of the Holy Ghost as you experience the shock of this revelation. You can quit begging and praying out of desperation. With God's divine will, all things are possible!

The Kingdom reveals itself when the Divine and human wills collide. You must understand that God's will *is* done! Something powerful happens when the human will is postured to receive the divine will of God. The struggle ceases instantly! Remember Jesus/Yahshua in the Garden of Gethsemane? The human and divine wills collided, and the will of the Father was the final word. Christ fervently prayed to the Father, "Let this cup pass from me." After much anguish, he reconsidered his petition and spoke, "Nevertheless, not my will, but your will be done." God's will was done!

Matthew 16:19 (AMP) I will give you the keys of the kingdom of heaven; and whatever you bind (declare to be improper and unlawful) on earth must be what is already bound in heaven; and whatever you loose (declare lawful) on earth must be what is already loosed in heaven. In my personal life, the keys to the Kingdom have unlocked miracles that go beyond the scope of my faith. I am a man of great faith, but there are things that have not even entered my mind, let alone that I have faith for, that God has done for me. I have unlocked financial increase that goes beyond my upbringing and the limitations imposed by my environment.

This model prayer is the formula to effect answered prayer. It is the alignment of body, spirit and soul. This pattern accesses His presence and His will. By following this model, you will find that it is not necessary to pray for hours. Today, I was awakened by Holy

Spirit at 3:00 AM, and I received illumination on The Perfect Prayer. God, simply, requires us to be a conduit of His power and glory for us to receive revelation. I saw this outline in the spirit of my mind.

Our heavenly Father, hallowed is your name.
Your Kingdom is come, Your will is done,
As in heaven so also on earth...

1. Never ask for anything of personal nature when you first begin to pray. The first three lines of The Perfect Prayer are all about His name, His dwelling place, His Kingdom and ultimately, His will.

Give us the bread of our daily need...

2. Know that no matter what you pray God's will is already done as in heaven so also on earth. What you are asking for here is enough for today! This part of the prayer deals with your daily assignment. Now, you can ask for something because by now you have reached a place of serenity and not desperation. Many of our prayers become pleas of desperation. At this stage in serenity, you can ask for your daily needs. Do not ask futuristically; ask in the present, in the *now*. How much can you handle today? Christ said, "Do not worry about tomorrow for tomorrow will worry about itself." Ask for what you need now, not in the future.

...and leave us serene...

3. Notice the verbiage is calling for serenity as a result of allowing others serenity. You get from others what you give to them. Sow serenity and you will reap serenity.

Just as we also allowed others serenity.

4. This is when you sow or give unto others. This is the seed-sowing portion of your daily ritual. Begin by sowing seeds of peace; then, sow tangible seeds. *Give something away every day.* Sow into your man or woman of God at your local church. And remember that your pastor is the one who gives you access at 3:00 in the morning. Remember that he is the one who picks up the pieces when you fall apart. He gives his lives sacrificially and often is the last one to receive a blessing. All too often, I see people sowing their "special" seeds to the televangelist, while their pastor is struggling to pay the light bill for the church or faced with a daunting financial circumstance. You reap from the anointing you sow into. My friend, Dr. Murdock says, "You sow up for wealth and down for health." In other words, you sow a seed into your spiritual authority, and God will release financial increase. Sow a seed to a needy person, and

God's response is divine health. Serenity means tranquility, calmness, peacefulness, quietude, and stillness. Go to a homeless shelter and volunteer. Sow the seeds of kindness. The result of sowing seeds of peace will result in the next portion of the prayer.

> *...and do not pass us through trial,*
> *except separate us from the evil one.*

5. The fifth portion of the formula is when we ask to be separated from the evil one. It is easy to blame Satan for everything, but the truth of the matter is, he is not omnipresent and cannot be at all places at all times. The separation has to do with the evil within each of us. We are born with a sin nature, and it is obvious that one of the first characteristics of each of our personalities is when, as children, we become defiant to what is right. Consecrate your heart to do good, which is the absence of evil. The only way to be separate from evil is to do good. Then, you will seal the prayer with the recognition of His Kingdom and authority.

> *For yours is the Kingdom,*
> *the power and the glory,*
> *to the end of the universe of all the universes.* ***Amen***

6. The glory is the place that houses everything you could ever need, want or desire. It is the warehouse of the unseen. Remember, with God's divine will, all things are possible. Jesus/Yahshua said, "Your heavenly Father knows what you need before you even ask." That is the divine will of God. He knows what we need because it is His perfect will. The key to unlocking these blessings that connect you to the divine will of God is to love God and worship Him.

What is worship? According to Strong's Concordance, the word worship comes from a derivative Greek word: *proskyneo*, which means (meaning to kiss, like a dog licking his master's hand); to fawn or crouch to, i.e. (literally or figuratively) prostrate oneself in homage (do reverence to, adore): worship.

WISDOM PRINCIPLE: WORSHIP IS
ABANDONED TRUST IN GOD'S PERFECT WILL,
HIS POWER, HIS GLORY
AND HIS KINGDOM.

Jesus/Yahshua said, "Agree quickly with thine adversary." This does not mean you are giving up. This is what I call wise

132

restraint. It comes into play when you have the ability to take down your enemy, but instead, you choose to restrain yourself to allow wisdom to win out. It is wise restraint rather than capitulation.

CHAPTER THIRTEEN
PRAYER AND WORSHIP

The woman said to Him, Sir, I see *and* understand that You are a prophet. Our forefathers worshiped on this mountain, but you [Jews] say that Jerusalem is the place where it is necessary *and* proper to worship. Jesus/Yahshua said to her, Woman, believe Me, a time is coming when you will worship the Father neither [merely] in this mountain nor [merely] in Jerusalem. You [Samaritans] do not know what you are worshiping [you worship what you do not comprehend]. We do know what we are worshiping [we worship what we have knowledge of and understand], for [after all] salvation comes from [among] the Jews. A time will come, however, indeed it is already here, when the true (genuine) worshipers will worship the Father in spirit and in truth (reality); for the Father is seeking just such people as these as His worshipers. God is a Spirit (a spiritual Being) and those who worship Him must worship *Him* in spirit and in truth (reality). The woman said to Him, I know that Messiah is coming, He Who is called the Christ (the Anointed One); and when He arrives, He will tell us everything we need to know *and* make it clear to us. Jesus/Yahshua said to her, I Who now speak with you am

He. Just then His disciples came and they wondered (were surprised, astonished) to find Him talking with a woman [a married woman]. However, not one of them asked Him, What are You inquiring about? *or* What do You want? or, Why do You speak with her? John 4: 19-27 (AMPC)

The first thing I noticed, when I delved into a deep study on this story, was the fact that God used a woman of ill repute to establish worship under the new covenant or New Testament. Jesus/Yahshua did not run from the woman at the well; he was kind to her and engaged in conversation with her. I grew up hearing the teachings of what a bad person she was and how she had 5 husbands, but Jesus/Yahshua opens up a whole new dimension of worship to her. The Bible says she left her bucket and ran to the town's people and told them everything. The fact that she had 5 husbands tells you she was searching for love in all the wrong places.

John 4:28-29 (AMPC) Then the woman left her water jar and went away to the town. And she began telling the people, Come, see a *Man* Who has told me everything that I ever did! Can this be [is not this] the Christ? [Must not this be the Messiah, the Anointed One?] Her uncommon encounter with the Messiah opened up an avenue of worship that led to the revelation that he was the Christ, the Messiah, the Anointed One. She had a thirsting deep within that only the unconditional love of a man could give her. Jesus said to her, "Give *Me* a drink... He was not afraid of her and his unconditional love opened her up to a divine moment.

In verse 26 Jesus said to her, "I who speak to you, am *He* (the Messiah). Ladies, quit looking to men to fulfill your emotional needs. Look to the giver of life, and he will give you water, and you will never thirst again...

You will never thirst for attention from a man again!
You will never thirst for respect from a man!
You will never thirst for verification from a man!
You will never seek validation from a man!
I am that water, I who speak am he, the Messiah!

Prayer as used in Matthew 6:9 comes from the Greek word: proseúchomai; to pray to God, i.e. supplicate, worship:—pray (earnestly, for), make prayer. The literal translation of prayer *is* worship! It's not that much about asking or petitioning, as it is about just worshiping in the middle of your mess. ...in the middle of your

5 husbands. …in the middle of your hardship.

Prayer is the agreement between man and the perfect will of God to work with the laws that the Almighty has pre-established. God is a God of order and works within the confines of His own laws. Often times, believers ask for things that actually violate and go against the laws of God and then wonder why they did not get what they asked for.

Worship is the final dimension! When we get to heaven, it won't be about feeding the hungry because there are no hungry in heaven. When we get to heaven, it won't be about clothing the naked because there is no lack in heaven! When we get to heaven, it won't be about money because God walks on streets of gold! When we get to heaven, it will be about worship! We will sing, "Holy, holy, holy, LORD God Almighty, Who was, Who is and is to come." And we will worship Him forever.

One of my favorite passages is: Psalm 119:165 (KJV) Great peace have they which love thy law: and nothing shall offend them. An aura of peace accompanies the individual who has no problems with God's boundary lines. Nothing can offend or upset the person whose mind stays focused on God's laws. Another passage says in: Psalm 16:6 (NIV) The boundary lines have fallen for me in pleasant places, surely, I have a delightful inheritance. God works with His own laws and expects His subjects to do the same. You cannot blame God for unanswered prayer. I have counseled many individuals who have become angry with God because He did not do what they asked.

I can remember watching my grandfather pray for hours at a time. I still have a vivid pictorial memory imprinted in my mind even after 20 years of his passing. His name was Leon, which means lion. I can say that I never saw the lion emerge from this tame, soft-spoken man. He would sit in his humble clapboard house in what should have been a dining room. His desk was pushed too closely against the curtains hanging shabbily around the paint encrusted windows, which gave light to the poorly lit room. His Bible was always open under the famous picture by Eric Enstrom entitled "Grace," a bearded, gray-haired peddler sitting at a table with a loaf of bread before him and his head bowed in prayer. Except for the long beard, my granddaddy could have posed for the picture himself. The warm rays of sunshine would pierce through the windows and bathe him in sunlight that would cause his white hair to shimmer and cast a heavenly glow around him. It was a moving and touching sight, but there was something missing from this picture. My grandparents were very poor monetary wise, but very rich in their faith. My grandmother was also a praying woman. I never stepped into her home that she was not in the kitchen wearing an apron cooking and baking. I can still see her silver hair combed flawlessly to the back of her head twirled into a bun. She had a special iron skillet that I called the *miracle* skillet. Much like the woman in the Old Testament that took care of the Prophet Elijah, her jar of oil never ran dry. My sweet grandmother's pan always had food enough to feed anyone who entered her home. There was never a question in my mind that my granddaddy was a godly man. In my young mind, I strived to be like just him, and I had a yearning and desire to have the stamina to pray for many hours because I figured that meant I was spiritual. I did grow up to be like my grandfather and became a man of prayer, ergo: this book.

Unlike my grandfather's humble prayer that was more of an *I'm-not-worthy* type of mentality, I somehow escaped those walls. I had the faith to bust down walls and mindsets of poverty and lack and still do! I could not reconcile in my mind how someone could pray so much and still be so poor. He was a brilliant man, but in his era, piety and humility were the great virtues to aspire to. He could quote a Scripture for any situation.

I decided to do things differently than what I had been taught, and I began to experience supernatural abundance in my life. I used to coach my young nieces, Miriam and Maranatha, to call me "rich" Uncle Thomas. My faith exceeded the perimeters of my upbringing because I dared to be different, and my faith made me fearless! I watched God bring hundreds of thousand of dollars into my life throughout the years that have totaled into millions. Through my prayer life, I have watched God empower me to buy a piece of land for 200 thousand dollars and sell it for over a million dollars.

When I was newly married at 22 years old, my wife and I purchased our first home, which was newly built, and we sold it to move to a bigger house with a pool on the golf course. We later sold that house and moved into a prestigious, gated community on the golf course into a home that was worth over 1.2 million dollars. We did not pay that of course, but our prayers of prosperity and faith have produced great increase and blessing in our lives, a huge contrast between my grandfather and me. I wish he could have lived to see what the power of godly prosperity, through prayer and sowing, has yielded in my life. I don't want to make it sound like life has been easy for my family and me. At present, we are facing the perfect storm regarding our home. Until God brings about the miracle, I believe He can and will do, our home could be foreclosed. I won't lie to you and say that I am never fearful of the impending foreclosure, but I choose to believe that God is able to do exceedingly, abundantly above what we can, or think or imagine! I believe His word is true and forever settled in heaven. We have been riding out this storm for the past few years, and there have been many close calls regarding foreclosure, but God has thwarted the plans of the enemy, and we are still here. I am living The Perfect Prayer for the Perfect Storm, and somehow, I know we're going to get through it! We will come out on top as we always have through every storm. The fact that I know that I am in God's perfect will lets me know that God is behind any storm in my life.

As long as Jesus/Yahshua is in the boat with you, it's not going anywhere! I will not rebuke the enemy because I know that my steps are ordered of the LORD, and what I'm going through is part of my destiny. Joseph had to go from the pit to the prison to the palace! If he had not been thrown in prison, Potiphar would have never known he was an interpreter of dreams. It was a setup by God all along! Even when he was thrown into a pit by his own brothers, it was all part of God's plan. Be encouraged! If you're going through a difficult situation, don't fret; put your trust in the LORD!

"Grace" by Eric Enstrom

Chapter Fourteen
Prayer of Prosperity

My dad died at a very young age; he was only 46 years old. He was not a believer until the last few months of his life. I look back at his life now and realize how young he actually was. At the time, I thought he was an old man who had lived a full life. I was a young teenager, about to graduate from High School. He was not a practicing Christian, but he was definitely a believer! He believed in the principles of sowing and reaping. He would often take from what we had and give it to the less fortunate. He once purchased a brand new refrigerator. I can still remember it was a beautiful Harvest Gold, Sears Kenmore! We were so excited because it had the ice and water dispenser on the exterior of the door. Within a few months, he learned of a person who was in need, and he took our Kenmore and gave it to the family.

He was a hard worker and a good provider for my mother and their seven children. Four boys and three girls, and I was the middle child. We were not rich; and at times, we felt poor, but we never lacked for anything. We were faithful to our local church and never missed any services. Sunday School, midweek service; we were there, and my mother always had money to put into the plate. I remember, she would sneak into my father's wallet after he had fallen asleep or passed out drunk. She would take cash and give tithes and offerings to our church. He would pretend that he did not know; and much of the time, he was clueless because he was a heavy drinker. Nevertheless, I remember the times when money would get tight, he would ask my mother, "Honey, have you given some money to the church?" He would then freely give her money to sow a special seed offering to the church because he knew that God's principles of prosperity work.

He may not have had a great prayer life or even known Christ in the traditional sense, but he always encouraged us to go to church and to listen to our mother, who would teach us from the Bible and pray with us each evening before bed. My father was able to unlock blessings and increase that my precious granddaddy never realized, even with his fluent prayer life.

The Perfect Prayer packs an arsenal of power to destroy poverty, sickness and disease. You don't have to ask for these things; they are the underlying fringe benefit of the prayer. The word fringe reminds me of the Tzitzits or tassels that hang on the four corners of my Tallit (Jewish Prayer Shawl). Numbers 15:38-39 (KJV) Speak unto the children of Israel, and bid them that they make them fringes in the borders of their garments throughout their generations, and that they put upon the fringe of the borders a ribband of blue: And it shall be unto you for a fringe, that ye may look upon it, and remember all the commandments of the Lord, and do them; and that ye seek not after your own heart and your own eyes, after which ye use to go a whoring... This is the very "hem" that the woman with the issue of blood in the New Testament touched. She pushed her way through the crowds and was obviously crawling because she reached up and could only reach the hem or the fringe of Jesus' Tallit. Jesus/Yahshua asked his disciples, "Who touched me?" The disciples must have chuckled among themselves because there were throngs of people on every side, but Jesus/Yahshua perceived that virtue had been pulled from him. And of course, we know that she was healed instantly! This is prosperity in your health! The wealth transfer is not just about money; it is about a transference of wealth of knowledge, wisdom and the miraculous. That's the mindset of kings!

Jeremiah 11:1-5 (KJV) The word that came to Jeremiah from the Lord, saying, Hear ye the words of this covenant, and speak unto the men of Judah, and to the inhabitants of Jerusalem; And say thou unto them, Thus saith the Lord God of Israel; Cursed be the man that obeyeth not the words of this covenant, Which I commanded your fathers in the day that I brought them forth out of the land of Egypt, from the iron furnace, saying, Obey my voice, and do them, according to all which I command you: so shall ye be my people, and I will be your God: That I may perform the oath which I have sworn unto your fathers, to give them a land flowing with milk and honey, as it is this day. Then answered I, and said, So be it, O Lord. Are you ready to move into your land flowing with milk and honey? Are you weary of being subject to the power of circumstances and human weaknesses? Do you possess a deeper hunger for more of God's presence in your life? Are you ready to rule with power, authority and dominion? If you are ready, allow me to welcome you to the gathering of kings! Welcome to the courts of the LORD! Welcome to a time for kings! Long live the kings of the kingdom! I could not write the chapter on prosperity without moving into the mindset of kings. If Yahshua is the King of kings and we are called to be kings, then it's time for the gathering of kings!

Romans 5:17 (AMP) For if by the trespass of the one (Adam), death reigned through the one (Adam), much more *surely* will those who receive the abundance of grace and the free gift of righteousness reign in [eternal] life through the One, Jesus Christ. It is very difficult for many to move from their poverty mentalities like that of my grandfather who prayed more than any other human I know. It's hard to go from thinking like a chicken to soaring like an eagle, but this passage secures your position in the kingdom of kings. I have never seen an impoverished king. Kings live off the wealth of the kingdom.

Be encouraged; once the storm has passed, you will come out ahead. The Bible says that the children of Israel left Egypt after 400 years of slavery with all the gold and silver, and there was not a feeble one among them! That's one of the remarkable times when the wealth of the wicked was transferred to the righteous.

Proverbs 13:22 (AMP) A good man leaves an inheritance to his children's children, And the wealth of the sinner is stored up for [the hands of] the righteous. Let me share with you briefly just a few passages of the dynasty you are a part of, being a king of the kingdom. There have been six wealth transfers in the Scriptures, and I believe we will be the seventh! Abraham, Isaac, Jacob, Israel, Joseph, and Solomon all received supernatural wealth transfers.

In her book titled Psych, The Psychology of Money, Rebecca Turner, my dear friend and financial advisor wrote that there is no perfect investment, and I could not agree more! However, I have seen a consistency in the principles of tithing, sowing and reaping. These are tried and true principles, but they are also subject to a person's integrity and faith.

I was reading the news online and ran across the story of a woman who woke one morning and had over a million dollars in her bank account. Granted, it was an internal bank error that was not discovered until a year later, and she was forced to return it. Nevertheless, I thought about how a supernatural wealth transfer could happen that simply. In the kingdom of the Living God, there is no lack; there is no poverty, and there is only abundance! Psalm103:19 (KJV) The Lord hath prepared his throne in the heavens; and his kingdom ruleth over all. That is the dynasty that you are privileged to be a part of! Psalm 96:10 (AMP) Say among the nations, "The LORD *reigns*!"

There is no question, as believers, we belong to a kingdom. Isaiah 43:15 (KJV) I am the LORD, your Holy One, the creator of Israel, *your King*. In the Old Testament, God called Israel to be a kingdom of kings and priests and a holy nation. If you are skeptical at this point because this is Old Testament teaching, Jesus/Yahshua said in Mark 1:15 The *time is fulfilled*, and *the kingdom of God is at hand*; repent, and believe in the gospel. He was declaring the kingdom of God, and he also said the kingdom of God is within us.

You cannot perceive the Kingdom mindset unless you are born anew. I'm not talking about getting saved; I'm talking about *thinking* differently. You must renew your mind, your thinking, and begin thinking like a king instead of a pauper. You have to be born anew in your mindsets, in your ideals, in your goals, in your dreams and aspirations.

Did you have a dream that has never been realized? Have your hopes been dashed by some devastating news? When you feel like you can't go another day, remember you are a king! When you go through the valley of the shadow of death, get through it like a king! When you cry, cry like a king! When you suffer, suffer like a king! When you die, die like a king!

Matthew 21:43 (NIV) Jesus/Yahshua said, "I tell you that the kingdom of God will be taken away from you and given to a people who will produce its fruit." (Author's paraphrase) It does not say people who *can* produce its fruit, rather, people who *will* produce its fruit. You have to be willing to do what it takes to produce!

Revelation 5:10 (AMP) You have made them to be a kingdom [of royal subjects] and priests to our God; and they will reign on the earth. When you start thinking and acting like a king, you move from the mindset of poverty to prosperity, and you begin to reign. You decide what you are going to tolerate! If you do not become vehemently angry at poverty and lack, you will never change. The mindset of the kings of the kingdom is the mind of Christ! You decide what you're going to put up with because you are a king!

Solomon was the richest man who ever lived. King Solomon was known for his wisdom because he was a philosopher. There was peace during his reign, and the kingdom prospered. The mindset of King Solomon was to resolve and reduce conflicts. When I first founded The Agreement Center, our slogan was "The problem solving church." Proverbs 4:7 says, Wisdom is the principle thing... Solomon's was a problem solver. Problem solvers who solve big problems get paid big money! You really don't have as many problems as you have a lack of wisdom. Your lack of money is really a lack of wisdom. And the beautiful thing about this situation is Scripture says, "If any man lack wisdom let him ask of God who giveth to all men liberally." (James 1:5 KJV)

It's time for the body of Christ to begin solving problems and quit creating problems. It seems that the church is more concerned about proving someone wrong or on the "other side" than solving the problems. Withhold not, when it is in the power of thine hand to do it! King Solomon was arrayed with fine jewelry of gold and silver, much like the Queen of England. I ministered all over England over the course of several years and was blessed to tour London. One of the most impressive displays is found in the Tower of London. It houses the crown jewels and their worth is inestimable. Solomon wore what the ancient texts called amulets. These amulets are what the Scripture refers to when the Bible tells us to write the word and put it on our foreheads, around our necks and on the doorposts of our homes. The Jewish Mezuzah is a form of an amulet, which is posted on my front door entryway. Every time I walk through the door, I touch the Mezuzah and bring my fingers to my lips and kiss them. It is a form of honoring the Word, and to some may seem ritualistic, and I couldn't agree more. The ritualism of honoring the Word when I enter my home has subconsciously set a standard in my mind that kings reside here. I believe honoring the word as a king of the kingdom supernaturally sets a precedent for all who enter our home.

Kings must be well adorned with the amulets of the Word of God. The wealth of the kingdom is about to grow because I have planted the seed of the Word of God in you, and I believe you will now go out and produce! Remember Jesus/Yahshua said, "I tell you that the kingdom of God will be taken away from you and given to a people who will produce its fruit." Long live the kings of the kingdom!

CHAPTER FIFTEEN
SWEET HOUR OF PRAYER

Throughout my life I have watched people, pray and experience a hit or miss level of success; I have come to realize there must be a timing to prayer, thus the title of this chapter. I am convinced that there is a *sweet* hour of prayer when what you pray happens because you happened to be within the timing of what is known as the sweet hour of prayer. The sweet hour of prayer is linked to the time line of Holy Spirit. It is a portal in time that has opened up as I mentioned in chapter five. It is like the farmer who knows the perfect time to pick a fruit. He waits to pick it at its optimal time for ripeness. There is nothing sweeter than a perfectly picked fruit!

With all the hours of prayer my granddaddy sacrificially gave, it was evident his prayers, although pious and sincere, were not producing what they could have, if he had grasped the power of wisdom. I believe wisdom is more than just knowledge and information. It is the ability to perceive and to instinctually know when to make a move. Wisdom is not *getting-it-right* every time, it is about knowing how to resolve the issue after you stumble upon it or conscientiously chose to make a wrong choice. I know some very smart men, but they make some pretty stupid choices because they lack wisdom. Like my unbelieving, alcoholic father who experienced success directly related to his faith in God's Word, proving that *God's Word works for them that work it* and that wisdom is available to anyone who honors *her*. Proverbs 4:7-8 Wisdom is the principal thing; therefore get wisdom: and with all thy getting get understanding. Exalt *her*, and *she* shall promote thee: *she* shall bring thee to honour, when thou dost embrace *her*.

These principles apply to the just and the unjust because they are immutable laws of God. My father finally came to know the Lord Jesus/Yahshua as his savior, but the word was working for him even before he was saved. The word works for them that work it! The old hymn comes to mind about the timing of prayer.

Sweet hour of prayer, sweet hour of prayer,
that calls me from a world of care,
and bids me at my Father's throne,
make all my wishes known.
In seasons of distress and grief,
my soul has often found relief,
and oft escaped the tempter's snare
by thy return, sweet hour of prayer.
Sweet hour of prayer, sweet hour of prayer,
The joys I feel, the bliss I share
of those whose anxious spirits burn
with strong desires for thy return.
With such I hasten to the place
where God my Savior shows his face,
and gladly take my station there,
and wait for thee, sweet hour of prayer.
Sweet hour of prayer, sweet hour of prayer
thy wings shall my petition bear
to Him whose truth and faithfulness
engage the waiting soul to bless.
And since he bids me seek his face,
believe his word and trust his grace,
I'll cast on him my every care
and wait for thee, sweet hour of prayer.

It is truly the grace and mercy of the LORD that keeps us as we walk through the valley of our own shadows of death. The song says, "In seasons of distress and grief, my soul has often found relief and oft escaped the tempter's snare by thy return, sweet hour of prayer." It is truly the grace of God that actually takes the very things meant for evil and turns them around for our good. The very trials and difficulties from which we ask deliverance are the catalysts that move us into our sweet hour of prayer. It is the sweet, sublime timing of Holy Ghost, which yields the perfect answer for each perfect storm. Unfortunately, some do not make it through the storms long enough to move into the sweet hour of prayer. Still, there must be a formula or a path that leads to the sweet timing of Holy Spirit, so when we face seasons of distress and grief, our souls can always find relief and always escape the tempter's snare.

Can you imagine the peace, the calm, the serenity that someone who has endured a perfect storm, out in the middle of the vastness of the ocean, must feel? Another song comes to mind as I write this, although the writer of *It Is Well With My Soul* had a different experience and outcome to his perfect storm. "When peace, like a river, attendeth my way. When sorrow like sea billows roll. Whatever my lot, thou hast taught me to say, it is well, it is well with my soul…" That's perfect peace!

How would you like to be in the prefect timing of Holy Spirit every time you prayed? Don't you think your prayer life would shift from hopeful wishing to absolute answers? Can you imagine the endless possibilities as you prayed within the perfect timing of the Spirit? It would be as though you had a VIP membership to the vault of heaven! You would probably want to pray without ceasing. This does not mean you spend the majority of your time in your closet begging God for things. What it does mean is you move from your will to the perfect will of the Father.

Anytime you align your will with the perfect will of God, you are in prayer mode. Anything you say can and will be used against you… In the courts of the LORD, what you say governs what you get. Anything you say can and will be used for your good! This is why I often caution people about what they say because they don't realize their power and authority as Sons of God. We are made in the image, an exact replica of our daddy/ABBA, and He created everything that is by the power of His Word. Knowing this, we should watch what we speak. Our words have the same creative power that our heavenly Father's words had when He created all that is.

Sometimes, there is not enough time to call upon the elders of the church for prayer as the book of James admonishes. There will be times when you cannot assemble the intercessory group or the prayer-chain online. Sometimes, all you have are moments to make your requests known to God, and it is in these critical moments that you must be ready, *in* the perfect will of God, positioned and prepared to see your miracles come to fruition.

Prayer is more than petition. For some people, prayer is like being a medical doctor "practicing" medicine and hoping he has prescribed the right medication with the right dosage. I see prayer more like being a chiropractic doctor. As a spiritual chiropractor, it is my duty to help people align themselves with the perfect will of God. And after a few cracks, snaps and pops, you are put back into your original state. Now, you can engage your vision and focus on the answer!

Let's look at man's original status with God. The Bible tells us Adam walked with God in the cool of the day. No telling how many mornings or evenings Adam walked face to face with God, with his every need met because he was in the presence of the Almighty. Adam probably never made a single request to God, because God walked with him face to face. He knew and planned for everything Adam needed and wanted. The Father eventually saw the need that Adam had for companionship.

James Weldon Johnson, an American poet, penned a magnificent poem called The Creation. In his poem, he portrays God, not only as Creator of everything, but he imagines a motive for the whole of creation. I very much agree with the vision Mr. Johnson affords us in that God had something on His mind when He spent those six remarkable days creating the heavens and the earth. And on the last day, He admired all He had made. It seems unfathomable to think of God being so alone that He was lonely. However, if we truly believe that God made all that is, then we must be inclined to believe there was a time when God was alone and was not content to stay that way. The Bible calls God, the Ancient of Days because God has always existed. When God created, He was pursuing more than a hobby; He was craving relationship and fellowship. I mentioned in chapter 13 how the Father is seeking those that will worship Him in Spirit and in truth. And remember the word seeketh actually means to crave.

The Creation
James Weldon Johnson, 1871

And God stepped out on space,
And he looked around and said:
I'm lonely—
I'll make me a world.
And far as the eye of God could see
Darkness covered everything,
Blacker than a hundred midnights
Down in a cypress swamp.
Then God smiled,
And the light broke,
And the darkness rolled up on one side,
And the light stood shining on the other,
And God said: That's good!
Then God reached out and took the light in his hands,
And God rolled the light around in his hands
Until he made the sun;
And he set that sun a-blazing in the heavens.
And the light that was left from making the sun
God gathered it up in a shining ball
And flung it against the darkness,
Spangling the night with the moon and stars.
Then down between
The darkness and the light
He hurled the world;
And God said: That's good!
Then God himself stepped down—
And the sun was on his right hand,
And the moon was on his left;
The stars were clustered about his head,
And the earth was under his feet.

And God walked, and where he trod
His footsteps hollowed the valleys out
And bulged the mountains up.
Then he stopped and looked and saw
That the earth was hot and barren.
So God stepped over to the edge of the world
And he spat out the seven seas—
He batted his eyes, and the lightnings flashed—
He clapped his hands, and the thunders rolled—
And the waters above the earth came down,
The cooling waters came down.
Then the green grass sprouted,
And the little red flowers blossomed,
The pine tree pointed his finger to the sky,
And the oak spread out his arms,
The lakes cuddled down in the hollows of the ground,
And the rivers ran down to the sea;
And God smiled again,
And the rainbow appeared,
And curled itself around his shoulder.
Then God raised his arm and he waved his hand
Over the sea and over the land,
And he said: Bring forth! Bring forth!
And quicker than God could drop his hand,
Fishes and fowls
And beasts and birds
Swam the rivers and the seas,
Roamed the forests and the woods,
And split the air with their wings.
And God said: That's good!
Then God walked around,
And God looked around
On all that he had made.
He looked at his sun,
And he looked at his moon,
And he looked at his little stars;
He looked on his world
With all its living things,

And God said: I'm lonely still.
Then God sat down—
On the side of a hill where he could think;
By a deep, wide river he sat down;
With his head in his hands,
God thought and thought,
Till he thought: I'll make me a man!
Up from the bed of the river
God scooped the clay;
And by the bank of the river
He kneeled him down;
And there the great God Almighty
Who lit the sun and fixed it in the sky,
Who flung the stars to the most far corner of the night,
Who rounded the earth in the middle of his hand;
This great God,
Like a mammy bending over her baby,
Kneeled down in the dust
Toiling over a lump of clay
Till he shaped it in is his own image;
Then into it he blew the breath of life,
And man became a living soul.
Amen.   Amen.

Adam did not have to make his requests known to God because he was *one* with God. He simply allowed himself to be vulnerable and showed his true emotions and feelings because there was nothing to hide from his Creator. God's natural intrinsic response was to fulfill Adam's needs even before he asked. And God saw that Adam was lonely, so He made Eve!

After God expelled Adam and Eve from the perfect environs of the Garden of Eden, they had to, now, communicate to God what they were feeling and what they needed. God was their supplier and always would be, but while they were in the Garden, they never had to voice their wants or needs. When Adam ate of the forbidden fruit, it was God who sought him out and called for him asking, "Adam, Adam, where are you?" As much as we may think we are chasing after God or seeking him, in reality God is chasing us.

2 Chronicles 16: 9 (KJV) For the eyes of the LORD run to and fro throughout the whole earth, to shew himself strong in the behalf of *them* whose heart *is* perfect toward him.   God is not running away from us, so we'll chase after Him. God has always been in loving pursuit of His children. When God found out Adam and Eve had eaten of the tree of knowledge of good and evil, He simply walked the gardens calling out Adam's name. There will be times when you must be still and know that He is God. Sometimes, you have to stop what you are doing and simply wait on the LORD to find you.

Prayer is not a way to make God do what we want, need or desire. I believe God wants the best for His children before we even ask for anything, but He will not be manipulated. Prayer changes *us* not God! I grew up hearing that prayer can change anything. Prayer doesn't change things; it changes us!

When God called Abraham and Sarah, they were two different people with two different names. God added the letter "H" to their names and Abram became Abraham and Sarai became Sarah. God was essentially engrafting His name, His initials, His character, His authority and His honor into Abraham and Sarah. The letter "H" is one of the four letters in the most holy name of God, which is known as the Tetragrammaton.

The fifth letter in Hebrew has a numeric value of "5." This number represents the "grace" and "goodness" of YAHVEH. Grace and love are two of the preeminent characteristics of God. All of God's works are characterized by His grace and all of God's ways are characterized by His love. Essentially, God was placing His favor upon Abraham and Sarah by engrafting this portion of His most Holy Name in their names.

The word "name" in Hebrew means: authority, character and honor. The four letter name of God represents His authority, character and His honor. The four points of the cross that Jesus/Yahshua was crucified upon represents the Tetragrammaton. The four-letter word, "INRI" was written on the *titulus* or the paper that was nailed above the head of Christ while on the cross, which stood for "Yahshua, King of the Jews."

In the New Testament, God introduces a high priest named Melchizadek, who had no father or mother. He was a created being and was the first of all High Priests. This is why Christ came as a king fashioned in the order of Melchizedek.

Psalm 110:7 (KJV) He shall drink of the brook in the way: therefore shall he lift up his head. David was writing prophetically of the coming Messiah. Melchizedek means a king of righteousness; the right; natural, moral or legal prosperity. As believers, we have the right to natural, moral and legal prosperity. The Messiah came in the order of Melchizedek to establish the wealth of God's government and kingdom.

Abraham did one simple thing that paved the path for God's reward system for us all. He tithed to King Melchizedek! He established a reward system and a fail-safe guarantee of protection along with surveillance provided by thousands times ten thousand angels. I believe the tithe is God's insurance of protection over us, and paying tithes is like paying the premiums. He uses the tithe to rebuke the devourer on your behalf. The devourer is not some monster or devil; it is the locust, the caterpillar and the swarms that often kill or decimate a farmer's crop. Malachi 3:10 speaks of tithes and *offerings*. When you pay your tithes, God rebukes the devourer from destroying your *fruit*. Three times a year the farmer would offer up first fruits in thanksgiving for the harvest and the increase. If the farmer had stolen the tithe, the devourer could eat up his crop, his fruit, and he would then be unable to offer anything before the LORD. There are people who believe in first fruits, but don't believe in tithing and some who believe the opposite. Nevertheless, God established a fail-proof system: pay your tithes; I'll rebuke the devourer; you will have a bumper crop increase, and then you pay your first fruits.

When you tithe to your local church in accordance to God's Word, you align yourself with the same order as Christ with Melchizedek. You may be thinking this is all Old Testament teaching, however in the New Testament, we find the same principle.

Hebrews 6:1-6 (AMP) Therefore let us go on and get past the elementary stage in the teachings and doctrine of Christ (the Messiah), advancing steadily toward the completeness and perfection that belong to spiritual maturity. Let us not again be laying the foundation of repentance and abandonment of dead works (dead formalism) and of the faith [by which you turned] to God, with teachings about purifying, the laying on of hands, the resurrection from the dead, and eternal judgment and punishment. [These are all matters of which you should have been fully aware long, long ago.] If indeed God permits, we will [now] proceed [to advanced teaching].   For it is impossible [to restore and bring again to repentance] those who have been once for all enlightened, who have consciously tasted the heavenly gift and have become sharers of Holy Spirit, And have felt how good the Word of God is and the mighty powers of the age and world to come, If they then deviate from the faith and turn away from their allegiance—[it is impossible] to bring them back to repentance, for (because, while, as long as) they nail upon the cross the Son of God afresh [as far as they are concerned] and are holding [Him] up to contempt and shame and public disgrace.

The time has come for the Church to mature and grow up! In this passage, we find a depiction of the lesser person blessed by the greater. In the one case, the tithe is collected by mortal men, and in the other case it is collected by the one declared an eternal being. One might even say that Levi, who collected the tenth, paid a tithe through Abraham because when Melchizedek met Abraham, Levi was still in the body of his ancestor. The Old Testament generation believed perfection could be attained by the Levitical priesthood on the basis of the law that was given to the people, but if perfection could be attained by the law, why was there still a need for another priest to come in the order of Melchizedek? Why didn't he come in the order of Aaron? When there is a change of the priesthood, there must also be a change of the law, and because of God's oath, Yahshua has become the guarantor of a better covenant: a better agreement, a better law.

Genesis 14:17-20 (KJV) And the king of Sodom went out to meet him after his return from the slaughter of Chedorlaomer, and of the kings that were with him, at the valley of Shaveh, which is the king's dale. And Melchizedek king of Salem brought forth bread and wine: and he was the priest of the Most High God. And he blessed him, and said, Blessed be Abram of the Most High God, possessor of heaven and earth: And blessed be the most high God, which hath delivered thine enemies into thy hand. *And he gave him tithes of all.*

Melchizedek not only received a tithe from Abraham, but he pronounced a blessing upon him. Abraham became engrafted into the order of Melchizedek, the order that never dies by the simple act of tithing! Since Melchizedek is greater than Abraham, he is also greater than the Levitical order, and his priesthood is more important. The Levitical priesthood dies, but Yahshua/Jesus has been made a priest *forever* after the order of Melchizedek. Hence the old order, which led to death, has been replaced by the new covenant of an everlasting kingdom, a kingdom that will never die.

Christ came under the auspices of the order of Melchizedek, king of righteousness, peace and justice. As we align ourselves with the new order and the will of the Father, we too come under righteousness, peace and justice. When you align yourself under the blood of Yahshua, who became the atonement for all, you need not be subject to the curse of sin and death. It was done for you! Yahshua, a High Priest in the order of Melchizedek, stands in righteousness, peace and justice for all who enter into the Kingdom of God. Are you beginning to see the connection: your lineage, your down-line if you will? When you pray, you have this heritage backing your every word!

During the Last Supper, Yahshua took bread and wine, just as Melchizedek had done with Abraham, and gave it to his disciples and explained what the elements represent. In the times of Melchizedek, these elements represented Shekinah (the *chabad* glory of God) and the beloved bridegroom; and now, they represent the body and blood of Christ the Messiah. Christ was symbolically ratifying the new covenant that was about to be sealed with his own blood because every testament, every covenant, had to be sealed with blood. With the new order and new priesthood came a new mantle of multiplication that is supported by the principles of tithes and offerings. Many people believe for what they pray, all the while ignoring the principles of tithes and offerings, and expect their prayers to be answered. Give us this day our daily bread... Everything that pertains to life and godliness is yours!

CHAPTER SIXTEEN
THE FIVE ELEMENTS OF PRAYER

Picture in your mind the Son of God praying The Perfect Prayer and teaching his disciples to do the same. The Bible says that he has experienced everything that we have ever been through or will ever go through. Postured in humility, when the time came to carry out his Father's will, he acquiesced by abject obedience.

Let's look at the Aramaic translation of The Perfect Prayer once again. *Our heavenly Father, hallowed is your name. Your kingdom is come, your will is done, as in heaven so also on earth. Give us the bread of our daily need and leave us serene, just as we also allowed others serenity. And do not pass us through trial except separate us from the evil one. For yours is the Kingdom, the power and the glory to the end of the universe of all universes. Amen.*

This is a prayer of absolute faith and trust.

- It is a prayer of alignment.
- It is a prayer of direction.
- It is a prayer of financial provision.
- It is a prayer of repentance.

157

- It is a prayer of increase. This *is* the effectual fervent prayer!

James 5:16 (KJV) Confess your faults one to another, and pray one for another, that ye may be healed. *The effectual fervent prayer of a righteous man availeth much.* Everybody wants their prayers to be effective and to avail much, but how many believers actually confess their faults? I know a lot of people who have the "fervent" part down, but what use is it to pray fervently, if it's ineffective? You limit yourself when you do not adhere to the behavioral patterns of Holy Spirit. You may have changed your behavior on the exterior, but change must be evident from the inside out.

In this same book, James writes that some people pray amiss because they ask things of God at the wrong time and with the wrong motive. They approach the throne inappropriately and usurp the protocol of prayer, which begins by acknowledging the sovereignty and omniscience of the Almighty. Much supernatural power remains untapped because we pray amiss. James also writes that we are praying amiss because we are at war with our brother. Are you praying amiss because you harbor aught against a brother? Are you praying amiss because you refuse to admit your flaws and refuse to confess your faults?

James 4:1-15 (MSG) Where do you think all these appalling wars and quarrels come from? Do you think they just happen? Think again. They come about because you want your own way, and fight for it deep inside yourselves. You lust for what you don't have and are willing to kill to get it. You want what isn't yours and will risk violence to get your hands on it. You wouldn't think of just asking God for it, would you? And why not? Because you know you'd be asking for what you have no right to. You're spoiled children, each wanting your own way. You're cheating on God. If all you want is your own way, flirting with the world every chance you get, you end up enemies of God and his way. And do you suppose God doesn't care? The proverb has it that "he's a fiercely jealous lover." And what he gives in love is far better than anything else you'll find. It's common knowledge that "God goes against the willful proud; God gives grace to the willing humble." So let God work His will in you. Yell a loud *NO* to the Devil and watch him scamper. Say a quiet *yes* to God and He'll be there in no time. Quit dabbling in sin. Purify your inner life. Quit playing the field. Hit bottom, and cry your eyes out. The fun and games are over. Get serious, really serious. Get down on your knees before the Master; it's the only way you'll get on your feet. Don't bad-mouth each other, friends. It's God's Word, His Message, His Royal Rule that takes a beating in that kind of talk. You're supposed to be honoring the Message, not writing graffiti all over it. God is in charge of deciding human destiny. Who do you think you are to meddle in the destiny of others? And now I have a word for you who brashly announce, "Today—at the latest, tomorrow—we're off to such and such a city for the year. We're going to start a business and make a lot of money." You don't know the first thing about tomorrow. You're nothing but a wisp of fog, catching a brief bit of sun before disappearing. Instead, make it a habit to say, "If the Master wills it and we're still alive, we'll do this or that."

We are required to be in right order with God's plan for our lives if we expect answers to our prayers. When you ask God for a miracle, He gives you a directive. I believe The Perfect Prayer covers every physical, mental, emotional and financial need you could ever have. The patterns of the path to health and wealth are not visible in the natural, but are intrinsic to the spirit man. You cannot get there by good works; you can only get there by the Spirit of God. The Perfect Prayer allows your spirit man to guide you instead of your flesh.

I have divided the prayer into five parts. The opening stanza places you in the first of the five elements.

1. *Our Heavenly Father, hallowed is your name, your kingdom is come, your will is done as in heaven so also on earth.* The first four lines are strictly about His name, His dwelling place, His kingdom and ultimately, His will. Never ask for anything of a personal nature at this point. You should never go before the throne with petitions for yourself or anyone else without first giving honor to the name of the LORD. Why? His name bears His character, honor and authority. Next you must give honor to His domain: His kingdom, where His will is *the* only will. There is much more happening in the realm of the unseen than in the world we see with our eyes. Albert Einstein said, "What our minds cannot comprehend really does exist!"

2. *Give us the bread of our daily need and leave us serene...*

159

No matter what you pray, God's will is already done on earth as it is in heaven. Knowing His will is complete in heaven, you can walk in serenity here on earth. Serenity is knowing your needs are met and you are able to be a blessing to others to create serenity in their lives.

3. *Just as we also allowed others serenity...* Ask for your needs after having reached a place of serenity. Do not let desperation be the only motive for your prayer. When you have made this progression, you can ask for your daily needs. Do not ask futuristically; ask for *now*. How much can you handle today? Christ said, "Do not worry about tomorrow, for tomorrow will worry about itself." He also admonishes that our Heavenly Father knows what needs we have even before we ask. That is the divine will. He gives us what we want even when we did not know we wanted it nor needed it.

4. *And do not pass us through trial, except separate us from the evil one.* If you are separated from the evil one, it will become more evident in your actions and choices. A sure way to skip the test or trial is by sowing peace instead of strife. Jesus/Yahshua said, "Blessed are the peacemakers for they shall inherit the earth!" When you sow a seed in direct relation to the instruction of Christ's model prayer, you reap a peaceful, serene life. Sow seeds of peace every day. To be separated from the evil one is more than rebuking devils and demons; it is more about staying on the path of His perfect will for your life. The path of the righteous does not intersect with the path of the enemy.

Are we going to have trials and tribulations? John 16:33 (AMPC) says, I have told you these things, so that in Me you may have [perfect] peace *and* confidence. In the world you have tribulation *and* trials *and* distress *and* frustration; but be of good cheer [take courage; be confident, certain, undaunted]! For I have overcome the world. [I have deprived it of power to harm you and have conquered it for you.]

In 1873, a wealthy lawyer named Horatio Spafford scheduled a boat trip to Europe, to give his wife and daughters a much-needed vacation and time to recover from the tragic loss of their young son, a few years prior. At the very height of his financial success, the Great Chicago Fire destroyed almost every real estate investment he owned. He was a devout Christian and had agreed to travel to England with the famous preachers, Moody and Sankey. He sent his wife and daughters ahead of him while he remained in Chicago to tend to some unexpected last minute business. Several days later he received notice that his family's ship had encountered a collision. All four of his daughters drowned and only his wife had survived. With a heavy heart, Spafford boarded a boat that would take him to his grieving wife in England. It was on this trip that he penned those now famous words:

When peace, like a river, attendeth my way,
When sorrows like sea billows roll;
Whatever my lot, Thou hast taught me to say,
It is well, it is well with my soul.

It is well (it is well),
with my soul (with my soul),
It is well, it is well with my soul.

Though Satan should buffet, though trials should come,
Let this blest assurance control,
That Christ hath regarded my helpless estate,
And hath shed His own blood for my soul.

My sin, oh the bliss of this glorious thought!
My sin, not in part but the whole,
Is nailed to His cross, and I bear it no more,
Praise the Lord, praise the Lord, O my soul!

For me, be it Christ, be it Christ hence to live:
If Jordan above me shall roll,
No pang shall be mine, for in death as in life
Thou wilt whisper Thy peace to my soul.

And Lord haste the day, when my faith shall be sight,
The clouds be rolled back as a scroll;
The trump shall resound, and the Lord shall descend,
Even so, it is well with my soul.

Be careful for nothing; but in every thing by prayer and supplication with thanksgiving let your requests be made known unto God. And the peace of God, which passeth all understanding, shall keep your hearts and minds through Christ Jesus. Philippians 4:6-7 (KJV) Whatever you're going through at this very moment, God has made a way out. You will get through this storm; you will live and not die and declare the works of the LORD. It is well; it is well… God always turns every bad situation around for our good. You will soon look back at this moment and be able to give Him glory for getting you through.

5. *For yours is the kingdom, the power, and the glory, to the end of the universe of all universes. Amen.* Choose righteousness, peace and joy in the Holy Ghost for this *is* the kingdom of God. Romans 14:17 (KJV) For the kingdom of God is not meat and drink; but righteousness, and peace, and joy in the Holy Ghost. Everything you will ever need, want or desire has been given to you in the glory of His perfect will. There is no lack in His kingdom! When we choose God, we walk in holiness by virtue of His Holy Name. We take on His character, honor and authority when we become a part of the family of God through His name.

1 Peter 1:15-16 (AMP) But like the Holy One who called you, be holy yourselves in all *your* conduct [be set apart from the world by your godly character and moral courage]; because it is written, "You shall be holy (set apart), for I am holy." Because He is holy, we are holy. His **character** is His holiness; His **honor** is His Word, and His **authority** is His Spirit.

Chapter Seventeen
Weapons of Mass Destruction

The authority of the believer is a topic that has been written about by many a scholar and great theologians throughout the years. I am not going to delve too deeply into the matter; however, I believe there are some ambiguities that could use some clarification.

When I think of authority, I immediately think of colonels, generals and people in uniform. When I think of the word weapons, I think *weapons of mass destruction*. Don't ask me why, but that's what I see in my spirit. Many believers are caught up in the warfare of words regarding our second amendment, the right to bear arms. And they are going out by the droves arming themselves with guns, semiautomatic rifles and an arsenal of weaponry because, as they argue, "We have to protect ourselves!"

Growing up, my father always had a plethora of guns and rifles in our house; albeit, I have never liked them because I've read too many stories of the empty barrel killing innocent people. In fact, with four boys, there was always an abundance of bb-guns, bows and arrows and plenty of water guns. I recall one incident, when my brother was taunting one of my sisters with a pellet gun that was supposedly empty. He aimed at her heart and fired, and to this day she bares the mark of a pellet in her chest that was never removed. Consequently, I acquired a bad taste in my mouth for weapons and decided right then, guns were not for me. However, something in my spirit, even at a young age, moved me to believe that God was and would be my source of protection. One of the first passages of Scripture I memorized was Psalm 91. "He that dwelleth in the secret place of the Most High, shall abide under the shadow of the Almighty..." I felt so secure and protected every time I quoted this Scripture, and I still do! Needless to say, I gained a different perspective of weapons, which instead opened up an entire dimension of spiritual weaponry.

The first weapon I learned to use was the power of the Word of God. There is no prequalification, no target practice, just speak the Word and "bang!" Of course, prayer is a weapon all on its own, but when coupled with the Word or with different spiritual weapons, it goes from handgun to *weapons of mass destruction*!

I mentioned earlier in the book that I am Jewish, and as a practicing Jew, I wear a prayer shawl or tallit when I pray. This is a powerful weapon that is created by simply tabernacling with Holy Spirit and praying the LORD'S Prayer and the Shema under the tallit.

In Israel, they have what is called or known as the iron dome that protects them from the many enemies launching attacks against them. When an enemy launches an air assault, the iron dome detects the assault and sends out a missile to destroy the bomb in the air. It reminds me of the scripture, "No weapon formed against you shall prosper..." The IDF (Israeli Defense Force) thwarts the attacks and keeps Israel safe. Two years ago, I was praying and the LORD gave me nine Scriptures that formed a spiritual iron dome for our homes.

GOD'S IRON DOME FOR YOUR HOME

1. PSALM 91:4 HE WILL COVER YOU *AND* COMPLETELY PROTECT YOU WITH HIS PINIONS, AND UNDER HIS WINGS YOU WILL FIND REFUGE; HIS FAITHFULNESS IS A SHIELD AND A WALL.
2. DEUTERONOMY 33:29 "HAPPY *AND* BLESSED ARE YOU,

O Israel; Who is like you, a people saved by the Lord, The Shield of your help, And the Sword of your majesty! Your enemies will cringe before you, And you will tread on their high places [tramping down their idolatrous altars]."

3. Psalm 3:3 But You, O Lord, are a shield for me, My glory [and my honor], and the One who lifts my head.

4. Psalm 5:12 For You, O Lord, bless the righteous man [the one who is in right standing with You]; You surround him with favor as with a shield.

5. Psalm 28:7 The Lord is my strength and my [impenetrable] shield; My heart trusts [with unwavering confidence] in Him, and I am helped; Therefore my heart greatly rejoices, And with my song I shall thank Him *and* praise Him.

6. Psalm 33:20 We wait [expectantly] for the Lord; He is our help and our shield.

7. Psalm 59:11 Do not kill them, or my people will forget; Scatter them *and* make them wander [endlessly] back and forth by Your power, and bring them down, O Lord our shield!

8. Psalm 84:11 For the Lord God is a sun and shield; The Lord bestows grace *and* favor and honor; No good thing will He withhold from those who walk uprightly.

9. Psalm 115:11 You who [reverently] fear the Lord, trust in Lord; He is their help and their shield.

Make a copy of these Scriptures, and post it over your front door, and watch the miraculous power of God's Word begin to work on all who enter. The Word is a weapon and coupled with the ancient paths of wisdom, it becomes a spiritual scud missile thwarting every weapon formed against you.

The Israelites relied on spiritual weapons often when the battle was too great. There were times when the raising of Moses' arms gave them victory over their enemies. Other times, they simply went in, and God had already caused their enemies to self-destruct. There will be battles that we cannot fight with our natural resources that will require a spiritual action. The walls of Jericho fell at the blast of the shofar and the shouts of God's people. The shofar is a powerful weapon that few understand or have ever experienced. The frequencies coming from the sounds of a shofar (ram's horn) cut through the atmosphere like an arrow of deliverance.

There is power in the simple act of partaking in the LORD'S Supper. It can be a powerful weapon for healing. One of my nieces was deathly ill and was laid up in a hospital bed in the ICU. I took a piece of bread and a drink of some sort, (we used what was available), and she walked out of the hospital the next day!

There are multiple weapons available for different things. The weapon of worship is the greatest warfare you can produce against the enemy. In my first book, The Agreement, I wrote of the W-A-R we can produce with our worship. Just simply **W**orship **A**nd **R**ejoice! That is a weapon of mass destruction! When you open your mouth and begin to worship and sing the song of the LORD in the midst of your circumstances, the heavens open up, and there's no stopping the glory of God. The writer of the beautiful song, It Is Well, wrote the song under much duress.

A gentleman in our church, Raymond Edwards, asked for prayer for a coworker who went in for surgery and did not come out of the anesthesia. He was in a coma for two weeks. We prayed and the LORD spoke to Raymond to take a CD player and to play one of my early morning worship CDs. The wife of the man in the coma was not familiar with worship, but appreciated the beauty of the music and the soothing atmosphere it created. Little did she know that the frequencies in that ICU room were being charged by the glory of God. The man woke up the following day! Sometimes a decision can change your dire circumstances quicker than prayer. (For a list of all my worship CDs, go to www.theagreementcenter.com)

There are a plethora of weapons of mass destruction at your disposal; it is simply a matter of knowing which one to use and when. The Spirit of the LORD will direct you; just open your heart and ears. When you ask God for a miracle, He will give you a directive. You have to do whatever it is He commands you to do, even if it is illogical. Naaman was instructed to go jump in the river, and he was incensed and angry! And yet, it was the weapon of mass destruction for the issues he was facing.

II Kings 5: 9-14 (AMP) So Naaman came with his horses and chariots and stopped at the entrance of Elisha's house. Elisha sent a messenger to him, saying, "Go and wash in the Jordan seven times, and your flesh will be restored to you and *you will* be clean." But Naaman was furious and went away and said, "Indeed! I thought 'He would at least come out to [see] me and stand and call on the name of the Lord his God, and wave his hand over the place [of leprosy] and heal the leper.' Are not Abana and Pharpar, the rivers of Damascus [in Aram], better than all the waters of Israel? Could I not wash in them and be clean?" So he turned and went away in a rage. Then his servants approached and said to him, "My father, if the prophet had told you *to do some* great thing, would you not have done it? How much more then, when he has said to you, 'Wash, and be clean?' So he went down and plunged himself into the Jordan seven times, just as the man of God had said; and his flesh was restored like that of a little child and he was clean. Never underestimate the instruction or directive of a man or woman of God. Oftentimes, Christians look for the way of sacrifice instead of the way of obedience. They believe if they make some great sacrifice or give away something really huge God will respond. Again I assert, God is not looking for perfection, He's looking for precision. How precisely can you do what He has asked you? If it means jumping in a muddy river seven times or seventeen times to get your healing, wouldn't you do it?

WISDOM PRINCIPLE: AN INSTRUCTION FROM A MAN OF GOD IS NEVER A SUGGESTION.

One of the most powerful weapons of mass destruction that is often overlooked is the power of agreement. My first book is subtitled: Unlocking the Favor of God because when you come into agreement with the divine connections, you run right into the favor of God. God loves when we walk in agreement and unity. Psalm 133:1 (AMP) Behold, how good and how pleasant it is for brothers to dwell together in unity! Sometimes God has placed His answer to your prayer in the form of a relationship. You may be asking God to heal you, but you may be unwilling to accept a divine connection because you "think" you're not compatible with a particular individual. The power of agreement goes into affect the minute you touch and agree with someone.

I just received a text from one of our faithful and tithing church members informing me that their small grandson was vomiting and weak, and they were on their way to the emergency room. I prayed the perfect prayer and aligned myself with God's will and sent the Word to heal whatever was ailing the little guy. I set out to go about my business when I heard Holy Spirit say this required a weapon of mass destruction. So I grabbed my tallit and got on my face. Holy Spirit reminded me of an incident in my own life that took place last month. My daughter found a few lumps in one of her breasts, and a friend, who is a nurse, urged her to have it checked right away. We made the appointment with our family doctor, and he saw her the very next day. With the history of female issues she has had in the past, the doctor felt the need to see her straight away. My daughter went in for her appointment, and I was overcome with fear. My mind began to race and I thought, what if she has tumors or cancers, or something incurable? I began to cry out to the LORD with a loud voice. I got under my tallit and began to speak the Word and wept aloud until I could no longer cry. She got her report the same day, and everything came back negative! When I prayed for the little baby just now, I thought, "How would I want people to pray for my daughter as she faced the threat of cancer?" I got on my face and tabernacled with Holy Spirit and cried out on behalf of this little one-year-old boy. I prayed the Word, I got under the tallit, and the combination created the weapon that destroyed the sickness and attack against this little guy. I just received a text from the grandmother: "HalleluYAH! He's doing wonderful. We are leaving the hospital in 45 minutes. Shalom Peace."

Arm yourself with the weapons of your warfare, which are not carnal, but mighty through God to the pulling down of strongholds.

168

CHAPTER EIGHTEEN
PRAYING THE WORD

My dear friend, Dr. Mike Murdock, invented the Topical Bible, which is a powerful tool for focusing on needs for a particular individual, like The Topical Bible for Mothers, Topical Bible for Fathers, business men, etc. There are many books about praying the Word of God, and they are great for zeroing-in on a particular need or particular problem. Incidentally, I am a huge proponent of focus and the need to simplify your requests to the LORD. I encourage people to find one or two Scriptures that they can meditate on and focus their faith on. Sometimes, we over-complicate matters by bombarding ourselves with too much information. The psalmist wrote one psalm at a time! Brain overload can happen even with God's Word. I believe in praying the Word.

Psalm 91 is one of the most beloved and quotable psalms in the Bible. I have known this passage by memory since I was a small child. My wife helped my two children memorize Psalm 91 when they were just two or three years old. There is something amazing that happens with David's writing that I believe will help you understand the concept of praying, or should I say meditating on the

169

Word as you pray The Perfect Prayer.

Psalm 91:1-16 (KJV) He that dwelleth in the secret place of the Most High shall abide under the shadow of the Almighty. I will say of the Lord, He is my refuge and my fortress: my God; in him will I trust. Surely he shall deliver thee from the snare of the fowler, and from the noisome pestilence. He shall cover thee with his feathers, and under his wings shalt thou trust: his truth shall be thy shield and buckler. Thou shalt not be afraid for the terror by night; nor for the arrow that flieth by day; Nor for the pestilence that walketh in darkness; nor for the destruction that wasteth at noonday. A thousand shall fall at thy side, and ten thousand at thy right hand; but it shall not come nigh thee. Only with thine eyes shalt thou behold and see the reward of the wicked. Because thou hast made the Lord, which is my refuge, even the most High, thy habitation; There shall no evil befall thee, neither shall any plague come nigh thy dwelling. For he shall give his angels charge over thee, to keep thee in all thy ways. They shall bear thee up in their hands, lest thou dash thy foot against a stone. Thou shalt tread upon the lion and adder: the young lion and the dragon shalt thou trample under feet. Because he hath set his love upon me, therefore will I deliver him: I will set him on high, because he hath known my name. He shall call upon me, and I will answer him: I will be with him in trouble; I will deliver him, and honour him. With long life will I satisfy him, and shew him my salvation.

Pay close attention to the verbiage David uses. Something in this psalm has stumped me for years. There are three voices speaking in this psalm. The first voice professes his trust in the LORD, and another voice responds in declaration, the Almighty shall preserve him. Without obvious punctuation or warning, David shifts from third person to first. Something supernatural happens when we recite Psalm 91, which is perhaps the secret to its great success. The verbiage postures you and positions you as the originator of the word. It takes you from quoting to the word to declaring the Word as though it was your own words. "He that dwelleth in the secret place... I will say of the LORD, He is my refuge..." The psalmist then shifts from simply talking about God's abilities into the very spirit and nature of the One whom he is hiding under—God! God's Word became his word! David goes on to say, "I will set him on high because he has known my name..." When

170

you speak to your spirit man something shifts, and you recognize that you are operating in the authority and the character of God's Spirit and in the honor of His Word. It is then that you begin to partake in the divine utterance of the living, breathing, active Word of God.

Praying the Word is more than quoting Scripture; it is as if the words of God become your words. I call it the *inception* of the Word. I have heard many teachers share great revelation on the *con*ception of God's Word and becoming impregnated with it, but inception-*izing* the Word takes you to a deeper realm.

Hebrews 10:16 (NIV) This is the covenant I will make with them after that time, says the Lord. I will put my laws in their hearts, and I will write them on their minds. This is the act of inception-*izing* the Word! You don't just quote the word; you become the word, like Jesus/Yahshua. God's Word becomes your word.

By faith, we understand that God framed the worlds into existence. Faith is not the vehicle or tool to get things; instead, it is faith that gives you the understanding, the ability to comprehend the workings and the mechanics of the power of the Almighty. Faith enables us to understand the workings and mechanics of God's power!

Isaiah 55:11 (KJV) So shall my word be that goeth forth out of my mouth: it shall not return unto me void, but it shall accomplish that which I please, and it shall prosper in the thing whereto I sent it. Many people think that this means they can attach their will or whatever motive they desire to this and send the Word out like an arrow, and it will accomplish "what they want." God's Word is not a "hocus pocus" formula you can attach a desire to in order to manipulate circumstances to get what you want. Remember, God *spoke* the Word; therefore, it is God's Word. The beauty in recognizing this is God's Word is already *done*! The Word will not return void because it is God's Word flowing through you to accomplish what God sent it out to do from its inception. This is why Jesus/Yahshua taught the disciples to "pray in this manner." *Our heavenly Father, hallowed is your name. Your kingdom is come, your will is done...* Nothing, no one escapes the will of the Father.

The law of physics can help us understand something about God's timing. Mark 11:24 (KJV) Therefore I say unto you, what things soever ye desire, when ye pray, believe that ye receive them, and ye shall have them. I firmly believe the moment you pray, you have already received what you asked. All too often we pray and *seemingly* nothing happens. Here is where my elementary understanding of physics helped me comprehend. Physics explains the time differences between all stars and planets in space. Our time zones are quite different from planets that are millions of miles away. An epic event could take place here on earth, and we could actually fly into space and see it happen again in that space continuum. You may be thinking, "And this relates to my prayers, how?" If you are dealing with a deadly disease like cancer or any of the other deadly, contagious diseases, you might be near death, but in God's timeless zone, cancer and disease do not even exist! Our God is ageless and timeless. He is the Ancient of Days from everlasting to everlasting, Alpha and Omega, the beginning and the end. From God's point of view, you never reach the point of death. You simply transition from this realm to His realm. In His realm, there is no cancer! In His realm, there is no foreclosure! In His realm, there is no lack!

You do not have to beg, plead or make a deal with God. Just shift your mind into the mind of Christ and decree and declare God's Word as *your* word. You were made in the image of your Father; you are a king! Only a person of authority can make a decree. A king makes a declaration, and it becomes law! Start looking at your circumstances and dealing with life as a king because you are a king! When you win, you win like a king. When you lose, you lose like a king. When you deal with others, you deal like a king. Focus on the mindset of the Word, which is the mind of Christ. In this timeframe, things you decree may not appear to have transpired; however, within the timing of Holy Spirit, it is done! *"...Your will is done, as in heaven, so also on earth."* In other words, God will position you and move you into the time zone of heaven where you are already whole. This is the dimension of dominion! Perhaps, you have wondered why some of your prayers have gone unanswered. You may be thinking to yourself, "I tithe; I give offerings; I go to church every Sunday; I help the poor." It is God's will to answer every time you pray. Psalm 91:14-16 (KJV) ....I will set him on high, because he hath known my name...He shall call upon me, and I will answer him...and shew him my salvation. Look what it says, "He shall call upon me, and I *will* answer!"

Daniel 10:12-19 (NIV) Then he continued, "Do not be afraid, Daniel. Since the first day that you set your mind to gain understanding and to humble yourself before your God, your words were heard, and I have come in response to them. But the prince of the Persian kingdom resisted me twenty-one days. Then Michael, one of the chief princes, came to help me, because I was detained there with the king of Persia. Now I have come to explain to you what will happen to your people in the future, for the vision concerns a time yet to come." While he was saying this to me, I bowed with my face toward the ground and was speechless. Then one who looked like a man[b] touched my lips, and I opened my mouth and began to speak. I said to the one standing before me, "I am overcome with anguish because of the vision, my lord, and I feel very weak. How can I, your servant, talk with you, my lord? My strength is gone and I can hardly breathe." Again the one who looked like a man touched me and gave me strength. "Do not be afraid, you who are highly esteemed," he said. "Peace! Be strong now; be strong."

When Daniel humbly prayed and aligned himself with God's will, his prayer was heard and answered! The twenty-one day delay was due to interference from the Persian kingdom. Daniel no doubt was feeling like he was losing the battle because he was focused on the inaction of the present moment. All the while, God had sent the answer the moment he prayed; however, the answer was tied into the future. *"I have come to explain to you what will happen to your people **in the future**, for the vision concerns a time yet to come."* The answer was connected to future events and a time yet to come! The issue was not that the "devil" or the King of Persia held it back! This was inconsequential to the answer. It was all about timing!

The prophet, Daniel, had a vision about some strange animal-like human beings. Perhaps theologians have a philosophical view of what kind of creatures they were, but I've had my share of dealings with humans who acted like monsters. In his vision, Daniel sees a horn waging war against the saints, and the horn appeared to be winning the battle.

I was awakened at 4:00 am this morning, and I remember dreaming that I was preaching from this very passage in the book of Daniel. I believe in prophetic dreams and visions and frequently experience them! In my dream, I was preaching and quoting the passage, "Everything by prayer and supplication; let your requests be made known unto God." There were people whom I have not seen in years in the audience. One man in particular was shouting out while I was preaching. He was shouting verses that contradicted what I was saying, but I would quickly find Scripture that would agree with the contradictory passages and thwart his attempts at creating disorder and disagreement. In the midst of all the chaos, a woman began speaking loudly as though she was on drugs. She was babbling and speaking gibberish and using the LORD'S name in vain. She then began to criticize me directly and attacking the message God had given me. And I remember that out of nowhere a Scripture rushed into my thoughts. Matthew 7:21: (KJV) Not every one that saith unto me, LORD, LORD, shall enter into the kingdom of heaven; but he that doeth *the will of my Father, which is in heaven.*

Although, the woman knew the Scriptures and even used the Most Holy Name, YAHVEH, she did not prevail over the message God had given me. Much like in Daniel's vision, I was experiencing *...the horn waging war against me, until the Ancient of Days came and pronounced judgment in favor of the saints of the Most High, and the time came when they possessed the kingdom.*

It wasn't until the Ancient of Days came and pronounced judgment in favor of the saints that they were able to take the kingdom! The gavel has dropped, and the judge has spoken in your favor! You have been chosen; you get to walk away from your accuser while your accuser is brought to judgment.

The Bible says that Jesus/Yahshua is seated at the right hand of the Father ever making intercession on behalf of the saints. Allow me to pose a sensitive question to hopefully provoke you to think beyond your traditions and the traditions of men that have been passed down from generation to generation. If Christ is seated at the right hand of the Father making intercession for you and me, what could you or I add to that prayer? I am sure the very one who told the disciples; "Pray in this manner..." knows how to pray *the* Perfect Prayer.

Think for a moment about the motive behind Christ's requests and intercession on our behalf. The very nature of this intercession is rooted in selflessness because he is interceding for you and me! It's not about him! He's asking the Father on your behalf! This is the same Messiah who walked on this earth and in whom was found no guile, no envy, no jealousy or no threat. He was all about the Father's will. Christ is obviously much attuned to the right motive in all that he does. He is not asking for something on your behalf with the motive of sharing it or gaining advantage over you.

Many believers have the misconception and/or preconceived idea that prayer and supplication means to make *any* request or demand of God. I am sure you're probably thinking about, *ask anything in my name... believe that you have received...* and all the other Scriptures that lead you to believe you can ask for *anything*. I am by no means implying that you cannot ask or that there is not a time for asking, but the Father knows what we need even before we ask. I wonder how much of our "intercession" is really about God's will and how much of it is all about what we want. You wouldn't ask your underage child to pay the mortgage, and you wouldn't ask your parents to do your laundry after you have moved out on your own. Ok, not a great example, because I know a lot of people who still go to mommy's house to have her do laundry. But it's out of order and it's wrong, no matter how you look at it and no matter how sweet and loving mommy is. Look at what the Scripture says right before going into the LORD'S Prayer: Matthew 6:5-9 (AMP) Also, when you pray, do not be like the hypocrites; for they love to pray [publicly] standing in the synagogues and on the corners of the streets so that they may be seen by men. I assure you and most solemnly say to you, they [already] have their reward in full. But when you pray, go into your most private room, close the door and pray to your Father who is in secret, and your Father who sees [what is done] in secret will reward you. "And when you pray, do not use meaningless repetition as the Gentiles do, for they think they will be heard because of their many words. So do not be like them [praying as they do]; for your Father knows what you need before you ask Him. "Pray, then, in this way...

If anyone knows how to pray, it is the one sitting at the right hand of the Father. Jesus/Yahshua prayed for his disciples; he prayed for future believers, and he prayed his High Priestly Prayer.

John 17:1-5 (AMP) When Jesus/Yahshua had spoken these things, He raised His eyes to heaven [in prayer] and said, "Father, the hour has come. Glorify Your Son, so that Your Son may glorify You. Just as You have given Him power and authority over all mankind, [now glorify Him] so that He may give eternal life to all whom You have given Him [to be His—permanently and forever]. Now this is eternal life: that they may know You, the only true [supreme and sovereign] God, and [in the same manner know] Jesus/Yahshua [as the] Christ whom You have sent. I have glorified You [down here] on the earth by completing the work that You gave Me to do. Now, Father, glorify Me together with Yourself, with the glory and majesty that I had with You before the world existed.

The most important or pivotal words in this passage are when Christ says, "The hour has come..." The hour has come for what you have prayed for twenty-one days or twenty-one years ago to come to fruition! The hour has come, and God has ruled in favor of the saints, and He has given us the kingdom! Whatever you ask by prayer and supplication in accordance to The Perfect Prayer, God will do!

David had 364 requests recorded in Scripture, that's almost one for every single day of the year. Christ prayed when he came into his hour of glory. This was an hour that was linked to God's heavenly timing, not earthly timing. It was his time, his hour of a mission accomplished. It was Jesus/Yahshua's time to be glorified by his Father.

Both David and Yahshua knew about affliction. I believe we are living in a time when more people are afflicted than ever before in history, not only in third world countries, but in America as well. So many refugees around the world are fleeing oppression and persecution. If ever there was an hour or time of the afflicted, this has to be classified as a historical time in history. This is the season for those who have been ridiculed and persecuted. It is the hour of the underdog. It is the hour of those who have stayed the course and relented not to the pressures of this world. It is the hour of prayer! It is the time to call upon the name of the LORD!

I recently posted a prayer that came forth from a collection of Scripture I know by memory on Facebook. I had received a negative report about my situation with my house. I resolutely declared: *It is well with my soul. I put my trust in YAHVEH. Shema Yisrael Adonai eloheinu Adonai echad. Hear O, Israel, YAHVEH our God, YAHVEH is One. Avinu Malkeinu. Our Father, our King. No weapon formed against us shall prosper! I am the God that healeth thee, I am the LORD, thy healer. For the LORD God will help me, therefore shall I not be confounded, therefore have I set my face like a flint, and I know that I shall not be ashamed. I serve the God of miracles, and I believe in His word and His word is the final say. Who's report will you believe? We shall believe the report of the LORD/YAHVEH. Great peace have they, which love thy law/word, and nothing shall offend them. I will keep him in perfect peace, he whose mind is stayed on me. Fear not for I AM with thee; be not dismayed for I AM thy God. I will strengthen thee, yea, I will uphold thee with the right hand of my righteousness. My God is faithful and true. Trust in the LORD with all thine heart and lean not to thine own understanding. In all thy ways acknowledge Him and He shall direct thy paths.*

One of the members of our church received a negative report concerning her daughter who lives in Houston, Texas. She called me up sobbing that her daughter had been to the oncologist and was given two to five years to live. Her diagnosis was a rare stomach cancer with tumors covering her entire stomach. I prayed the Perfect Prayer with her, and she packed her bags and drove to Houston to be by her daughter's side. She logged on to her Facebook account and noticed I had posted a prayer on my wall that reflected my own personal crisis. She began praying the collection of Scriptures that had now become *her* prayer, *her* words, *her* declaration. For two weeks, she prayed this prayer every morning and stood in faith for her healing. A few days later, she received an email from her daughter and was astonished at the report. The doctors revised their results and informed her the rare cancer previously diagnosed had now been reduced to a simple case of ovarian cancer. In light of the rarity of the first diagnosis, ovarian cancer seemed like an easy, quick fix through surgery. Either way, she knew this was more than a crisis-averted-moment. This was a miracle, a signs and wonders moment! And it was changed by the power of a simple prayer and the declaration of God's Word. She shall live and not die and declare the works of the LORD/YAHVEH!

As I was finishing up the final edit on this book, the words were becoming more and more real. I prayed the prayer once again over the situation with my house. The anxious buyers that have been planning to move into our beautiful home scheduled inspectors of every kind; pest, slab, foundation, pool, roof, land engineers and a fence installer. They spent hours in our home, while we waited around for them to finish their negotiations. I was feeling very discouraged and fearful of where I would move my family. The following morning after the inspections, I awoke early and postured myself under my prayer shawl (tallit) and prayed the perfect prayer and asked God to thwart the plans of these opportunists trying to take our home. Within a couple of hours of my prayer, I received a text from our realtor stating that the buyers had backed out! After thousands of dollars of inspections and months of planning, the deal was off! God stopped them in their tracks! The perfect storm was silenced! I cried unto the LORD with my voice, and he heard my cries. Every storm has its run, and in the end, there is always calm, peace, tranquility and many times a rainbow.

Speak up! Don't be afraid to voice your cries of worship to the Father. The perfect storm does not have the final say for your life. Arise and courageously declare, *"Our heavenly Father, hallowed is your name! Holy is your character, honor and your authority!"*

Stand up on the bow of your ship and speak to the storm, "Peace, be still!" In the authority of the name, command that storm to cease and desist! And if the storm refuses to relent, listen for the voice of the master crying, "Come on and walk on the water with me. You will not fail; you will not fail!" Open your mouth and sing the song of the Spirit; give God all the worship He deserves, and stand back, and see the salvation of your God! Write the vision; make it plain; make it visible for everyone to see. Stop listening to the naysayers; stop listening to the sound of the 'horn of the beast.' God has ruled in your favor! This is your parade; march with your head held high. March while you can; march while there is yet the light of day, and declare your victory! Never give up; never give in, and know in whom you have believed. It is He who gives wings to your prayers as they ascend to the heavens. The storm has passed; the waters have receded, and the clouds have given way to the rainbow of His promise. And *this* is the victory that overcomes the world, even our faith!

"…Yours is the Kingdom,
the Power and the Glory,
to the end of the universe of all universes! Amen!"

BIBLIOGRAPHY

New International Version (NIV) Holy Bible, New International Version®, (NIV)® Copyright © 1973, 1978, 1984, 2011 by Biblica, Inc.® Used by permission. All rights reserved worldwide.

The King James 2000 Bible, Copyright © Doctor of Theology Robert A. Couric 2000, 2003 Used by permission. All rights reserved.

King James Version (KJV) Public Domain

The (ESV)® Bible (The Holy Bible, English Standard Version®) copyright © 2001 by Crossway Bibles, a publishing ministry of Good News Publishers. The (ESV)® text has been reproduced in cooperation with and by permission of Good News Publishers. Unauthorized reproduction of this publication is prohibited. All rights reserved.

New Century Version (NCV) The Holy Bible, New Century Version®. Copyright © 2005 by Thomas Nelson, Inc.

Authorized King James Version (AKJV) (KJV) reproduced by permission of Cambridge University Press, the Crown's patentee in the UK.

Amplified Bible (AMP) Copyright © 2015 by The Lockman Foundation, La Habra, CA 90631. All rights reserved.

Amplified Bible, Classic Edition (AMPC) Copyright © 1954, 1958, 1962, 1964, 1965, 1987 by The Lockman Foundation

International Standard Version (ISV) Copyright © 1995-2014 by ISV Foundation. ALL RIGHTS RESERVED INTERNATIONALLY. Used by permission of Davidson Press, LLC.

Number In Scripture by E.W. Bullinger, Published in 1967 by Kregel Publications, a division of Kregel, Inc., Grand Rapids, MI)

The Age of Aquarius by the fifth dimension, 1969 soul City Records Circa 1971 The Carpenters from the Album: Carpenters)

Netzarifaith.org The oldest known Bible Text Bar Yosef, Rav Yaakov, "Lord's Prayer in Ancient Aramaic." http://netzarifaith.org/netzari-faith/lords-prayer-in-the-ancient-aramaic (accessed June 01, 2010)

Walk on the Water With Me Authors, Dony McGuire, Ray Beban, Reba Rambo Copyright © 1992 Songs Of Rambo McGuire

Holy to YAHVEH Author, Terrye Goldblum Seedman Copyright

179

© 1996 Goldblum Seedman Corporation   All Rights Reserved
Published by Longwood Communications DeBary, FL

Sweet Hour of Prayer Lyrics by William Walford and Music by William B. Bradbury

MySpace.com Founders Chris DeWolfe & Tom Anderson. August 1, 2003. Beverly Hills , CA

King of Queens, *"Holy Mackerel."* CBS. Sony Production Studios. Culver City, CA. 7 Oct. 2002. Television

Could You Not Tarry One Hour? author, Dr. Larry Lea Copyright © 1987 by Larry Lea, All rights reserved. Published by Charisma House, Charisma Media, Charisma House Book Group.

The Tempest – Painting by Artist, Ivan Aivazovsky – Public Domain

Grace – Painting by Artist, Eric Enstrom Image by Wikipedia® is a registered trademark of the Wikimedia Foundation, Inc. a non-profit organization.

The Creation *by James Weldon Johnson, 1871* Copyright © 2005-2012 INTERNET ACCURACY PROJECT. All rights reserved

It Is Well Author, Horatio G. Spafford, 1873 – Public Domain

Merriam-Webster's Collegiate Dictionary. 11th ed. Springfield, MA: Merriam-Webster, 2003.

The Prayer of Jabez: Breaking Through to the Blessed Life. Wilkinson, Bruce. Sisters, OR: Multnomah Books, 2000.

The Psychology of Money Copyright © Rebecca D. Turner, 2011

SUPPORT THIS MINISTRY

Dear Friend,

I want to encourage you to plant a special seed of any size, today as the Holy Spirit leads you. Your seed will help me spread the Wisdom of God, establish and raise up Worshipers, and release God's strategies for wealth in the kingdom. As you sow, remember God's promise "…to do exceedingly abundantly, above what you can ask or think or even imagine."

Yes, Dr. Thomas! I am sowing with anticipation that God will perform His Word and multiply my seed! I know my seed will yield a great harvest. I know I cannot buy a miracle or buy special powers. My seed documents, in the eyes of God that I am in agreement with you and His word. I can expect a miracle of blessings in my personal life. I am sowing a seed in the amount of $_____ to spread God's Word. I call forth the harvest for the salvation of my loved ones and financial increase in my life.

Please send me your prayer request. I am in agreement that every time God blesses me, He will bless you!

BECOME A MONTHLY PARTNER

Join the revolution of worshipers! I know God has brought us together for such a time as this. He is gathering the remnant of worshipers and grooming them to become the glorious Bride. Your monthly seed can be the link between you and me. When you sow the seed of worship, it unlocks the unimaginable. Mail your seed and prayer needs to:

DR. THOMAS MICHAEL
C/O THE AGREEMENT CENTER
P.O.BOX 200367 ARLINGTON, TX 76006
Or visit us on our website and click the Donate button at the bottom of the home screen.

www.theagreementcenter.com

THE AGREEMENT *UNLOCKING THE FAVOR OF GOD*

In a society riddled with separation, divorce, and abandonment... People cry out, but cannot be heard. In a world where life has lost its sanctity and love has lost its soul... People bleed, but no one sees. Amidst the shattered wreckage of the American home... Another family dies, but no one cares, meanwhile, the God of Covenant yearns for unity and oneness among His own. From the bowels of heaven comes a cry for man to return to the way things were meant to be. "The Father seeketh such that will worship him in spirit and in truth..." God is calling for truth, realness, and genuine companionship with his people. In answer to this call, Dr. Thomas uses the mastery of writing to unveil the mystery of the most ancient of God's ordinances, The Agreement.

THE SECRET

A Kingdom where everything is perfect, sublime, and beautiful suffers a coup that disrupts the very foundation of its existence. The Three who rule in this Kingdom have never had an argument, a disagreement or a moment of jealousy; They rule and reign as one. Something cryptic is lurking about in many believers' lives. You cannot see it, smell it, or touch it; but most of us have felt the burn or sting of its far-reaching effects. It clings to its victim like an undetected mildew inside the walls of an otherwise immaculate room. It is there when they go to bed at night. It is a mystery that dates back to the first family on earth. What is it? It is a secret, a mystery, and mysteries must be discovered. ~Discover the reasons why many believers are plagued with sickness and disease, and suffer lack in many areas of their lives. ~Discover the secret of perfect living, free from haunting pasts.

THE LAW OF ORDER

Dr. Thomas brings to light a topic that has been obscured by religious fluff far too long; it is an ordinance as old as time...Tame the disorder around you and discover a life changing principle: The Realm of the Spirit is Order. The Law of Order will revolutionize your life and provoke you to eliminate chaos and disorder. Order is the sequential arrangement of things. God is a God of order.

www.ingramcontent.com/pod-product-compliance
Lightning Source LLC
Chambersburg PA
CBHW022006090426
42741CB00007B/919